SNAKEBITE!

ANTIVENOM
AND
A GLOBAL HEALTH CRISIS

CHARLES C. HOFER

TWENTY-FIRST CENTURY BOOKS / MINNEAPOLIS

Acknowledgments
The author would like to thank the many people who helped out during the course of this project. First and foremost, many thanks to Dr. Leslie Boyer for answering endless questions. Thanks to Dr. Alejandro Alagón for inviting me to his lab in Cuernavaca, Mexico, and the ranch in Pueblo, Mexico; to Stephane Poulin of the Arizona-Sonora Desert Museum; to Edgar, Melisa, and Roberto for their help in Mexico; and to Ray Morgan, Connie Choza, Dr. Carlo Valentino, Anna and Domenica and, of course, Gracie, for her moral support.

Twenty-First Century Books
A division of Lerner Publishing Group, Inc.
241 First Avenue North
Minneapolis, MN 55401 USA

For reading levels and more information, look up this title at www.lernerbooks.com.

Library of Congress Cataloging-in-Publication Data

Names: Hofer, Charles, author.
Title: Snakebite! : antivenom and a global health crisis / Charles C. Hofer.
Description: Minneapolis : Twenty-First Century Books, [2019] | Audience: Age
    13–18. | Audience: Grade 9 to 12. | Includes bibliographical references and index.
Identifiers: LCCN 2017046976 (print) | LCCN 2017048478 (ebook) |
    ISBN 9781541524798 (eb pdf) | ISBN 9781512483734 (lb : alk. paper)
Subjects: LCSH: Poisonous snakes—Juvenile literature. | Snakebites—Juvenile
    literature. | Antivenins. | Medical care—Juvenile literature.
Classification: LCC QL666.O6 (ebook) | LCC QL666.O6 H654 2019 (print) | DDC
    597.96/165—dc23

LC record available at https://lccn.loc.gov/2017046976

Manufactured in the United States of America
1-43367-33179-5/15/2018

CONTENTS

Venomous snakes live all over the world, and their deadly bites kill thousands of people each year, especially in regions such as sub-Saharan Africa, Southeast Asia, and South America. This deadly eyelash pit viper (*Bothriechis schlegelii*) lives in Central and South America.

INTRODUCTION
A DEADLY BITE

On a hot August night, three medical doctors settle in for a relaxing dinner after a long day's work. American physician Dr. Leslie Boyer and two colleagues have spent the day visiting a small hospital in Tanguiéta, a small village in the African nation of Benin.

At dinner the three doctors talk about the day's events and the work that lies ahead. They have come to Benin to train local medical workers and to help solve a health crisis that is ravaging this part of the world. The epidemic is snakebite, a health crisis that strikes young and old alike, killing tens of thousands each year across sub-Saharan Africa. This large, tropical region stretches across the continent south of the

People in Benin and other African nations experience hundreds of snakebites each year.

Sahara, the world's largest hot desert. The region includes the nations of Ethiopia, Nigeria, and Rwanda.

A cell phone rings. "I know you were just here all day," says a frantic voice on the other end. "But a little boy has just arrived, and he's desperately sick!" Within minutes the three doctors abandon their meal and are back in their Land Rover, lurching over the endless bumpy dirt roads that crisscross the sprawling Benin countryside. The journey back to the hospital in Tanguiéta will take an hour, and every second counts.

The doctors arrive shortly before midnight. Hospital workers swiftly escort them to a ten-year-old boy curled up in a small hospital bed. He is bleeding from his eyes, and he is going into shock, a medical emergency that causes basic bodily functions such as breathing to shut down. The boy is unable to talk or hold himself up. His abdomen is swollen too, suggesting that he might be bleeding from the inside.

To Boyer and her colleagues, the cause of the symptoms is obvious: the boy was bitten by a venomous snake. Such snakes use a dangerous

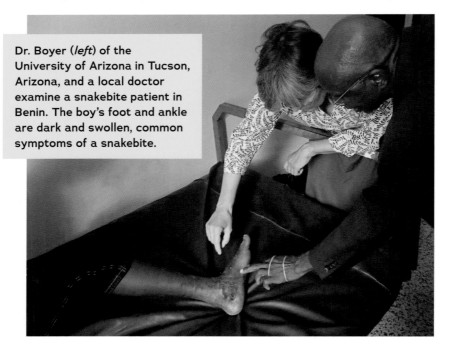

Dr. Boyer (*left*) of the University of Arizona in Tucson, Arizona, and a local doctor examine a snakebite patient in Benin. The boy's foot and ankle are dark and swollen, common symptoms of a snakebite.

biological chemical known as venom to ward off perceived threats. The venom can be deadly to people and other animals. In talking with the boy's family, the staff knows that the boy's bite occurred less than fourteen hours ago. His condition is getting worse with each passing minute. At the location of the bite, near the boy's ankle, the skin has turned dark. His ankle has puffed up with swelling. The snake's venom is spreading rapidly, coursing through the young boy's body and attacking it from the inside.

Small cuts on the boy's leg near the bite indicate that a family member or local healer tried traditional healing methods before bringing the boy to the hospital. These methods often involve cutting the wound so the snake venom will leak out with the blood. However, this causes an additional loss of blood and delays proper medical attention. The only lifesaving treatment for a venomous snakebite is antivenom. The medicine is created from the deadly venom itself. If doctors don't take action immediately, the boy will die before sunrise.

The hospital has already given the boy the only two vials of antivenom they had. But the medicine did not slow the effects of the snake's venom. Luckily, one of Boyer's colleagues has brought a personal supply of effective antivenom with him. Will this be enough? The clock is ticking, and the venom already has a significant head start.

The doctors carefully administer the medicine, using a needle to inject the boy with a higher dose and at a faster rate than is typical for antivenom. It's a dangerous way to deliver the medicine, but they have no other options. Time is running out.

The team steps back to watch the boy as the antivenom goes to work. If it doesn't work, nothing more can be done.

In less than an hour, the boy stops bleeding. His breathing returns to normal, and he sits up in bed. "My leg itches!" he exclaims. Everyone in the room breathes a sigh of relief. The boy is well on his way to recovery.

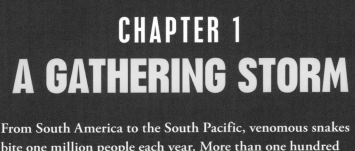

CHAPTER 1
A GATHERING STORM

From South America to the South Pacific, venomous snakes bite one million people each year. More than one hundred thousand people die from their bites, and many more are permanently injured. Worldwide, about four hundred thousand snakebite patients undergo amputation (removal of limbs from the body). Snake venom is aggressive, and it can destroy skin, muscles, and organs if not treated quickly. This kind of injury can be devastating to a family or community, especially in nations where medical care is limited.

In the United States and Canada, about ten thousand venomous snakebites occur each year. Of the people bitten by those snakes, only a small handful die. Usually hospitals in these nations are well equipped, and people seek help in time

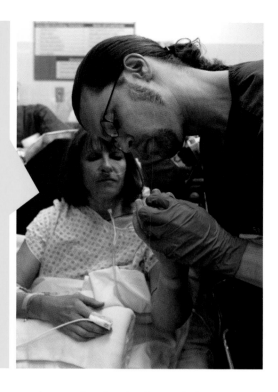

Dr. Sean Bush (*right*) treats a snakebite patient at Loma Linda University Medical Center in Southern California. The patient was bitten while hiking in Joshua Tree National Park. Bush specializes in snake venoms and treats about fifty snakebite patients each year.

to guarantee survival. In regions that are hardest hit by snakebites—such as sub-Saharan Africa or Southeast Asia—venomous snakes are plentiful but adequate medical care is not. Hospitals and other medical facilities may be underfunded, understaffed, and unable to treat snakebite victims properly. For some communities, medical facilities that can treat a snakebite properly can be several hours or a day's travel away. Following a venomous bite, every minute is precious as the deadly venom starts working its way through the victim. Delayed action in seeking medical help and proper antivenom treatment can have deadly consequences.

In rural areas of Brazil and Colombia in South America, for example, venomous snakebites kill up to five thousand people each year. In certain parts of Southeast Asia, the death rate can reach nineteen thousand annually. Venomous snakebites in India kill about

PROSTHETIC PROBLEM

According to the World Health Organization (WHO), thirty million people in low-income countries need prosthetic devices. This number includes those who have had limbs amputated due to snakebites, people who have lost limbs to land mines or other accidents, and children who were born without limbs. However, people in these countries often do not have access to affordable prosthetic devices or clinics and medical professionals trained in constructing, fitting, and adjusting the limbs. Prosthetic limbs must be replaced or repaired frequently, and many are made for a Western lifestyle. The limbs can't hold up to tropical climates or use in rural life and farm labor.

Several organizations are working to make prosthetic devices more available for those in low-income nations. Nia Technologies is a nonprofit based in Canada that has developed 3D printing technology to print prosthetic limbs. Nia has tested its technology in Uganda, Tanzania, and Cambodia. With the technology, a technician can create a limb in under two days. This cuts down on costs for the hospital and wait times for patients. Matt Ratto, Nia's chief science officer, says that he wants to fit eight thousand people in twenty low-income nations with 3D-printed prosthetics by 2022.

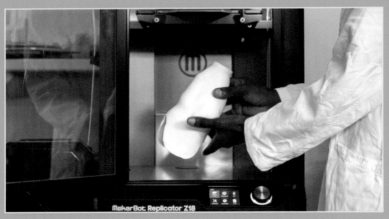

An orthopedic technology specialist works with a 3D-printed prosthetic limb at Comprehensive Rehabilitation Services of Uganda (CoRSU), an organization that works to improve the lives of people living with disability. Many in Uganda believe that losing a limb means losing a life, but CoRSU and other organizations are working to change this perception.

thirty-three thousand people each year. In sub-Saharan African nations such as Kenya, Ghana, and Benin, venomous snakes cause more than thirty thousand deaths annually. And these are all conservative estimates. The number of deaths from snakebites might actually be much higher, but it is difficult to know for sure. Not all cases are reported. Some victims may rely on traditional healing methods and never make it to a hospital. Other cases may go undocumented in hospitals that don't keep proper records of treatment.

THE VICIOUS CIRCLE

At the University of Arizona in Tucson, the College of Medicine is a vast, sprawling building that covers several city blocks. Tucked away six floors up, in a windowless corner of the building, is the VIPER Institute. (VIPER stands for Venom Immunochemistry, Pharmacology, and Emergency Response.) Boyer has dedicated her life to developing effective and inexpensive antivenoms. She is the founding director of the institute. Over her career, she has worked with a variety of venomous creatures, including scorpions, Gila monsters, black widow spiders, and venomous snakes—lots of venomous snakes.

The solution to the snakebite problem seems simple: provide effective antivenoms to the people and communities that need it most.

Boyer is an expert in snake and scorpion antivenom. She founded the VIPER Institute in 2007 to further research venoms and antivenoms and to try to solve the snakebite crisis.

However, the solution is not actually that simple. For Boyer and other researchers like her, rigorous lab work to develop antivenoms is only part of the job. As with any effective medicine, a dependable supply chain to reach the communities in need is key. For antivenom, this supply chain begins in modern research labs and moves to production sites in Mexico, France, South Africa, or Saudi Arabia. The journey moves to Washington, DC, and Europe, where policy makers and big pharmaceutical companies decide who will get the medicine and at what price. Finally, antivenom goes to sub-Saharan Africa, Southeast Asia, or another region affected by the snakebite crisis. There, the most difficult part of the journey begins as medical workers try to earn the trust of the communities that need help fighting this plague. This is not easy because many communities first turn to their own traditional methods, which are mostly ineffective against venomous snakebites.

For more than two decades, Boyer has helped lead the charge in the fight against the global snakebite crisis. As with other international health crises—such as Ebola or human immunodeficiency virus (HIV) and acquired immunodeficiency virus (AIDS)—there is no magic bullet or one simple solution. Like an octopus with many tentacles, the snakebite problem is complex with many contributing factors. Each requires its own specific resources to fix. Boyer calls this phenomenon the Vicious Circle.

"The Vicious Circle needs everything at once to be addressed," she says. "We need to have high-quality [antivenom] products available. We need to fund their purchase and distribute them to where they need to be. We need to train doctors and nurses how to use them well. And we need the general public to understand what's possible."

The Vicious Circle has several factors that feed the snakebite crisis. First are the communities in need. They are largely in regions where resources are scarce and venomous snakes are common. The communities are often rural, with local economies based on agriculture. Large portions of the population work in fields where

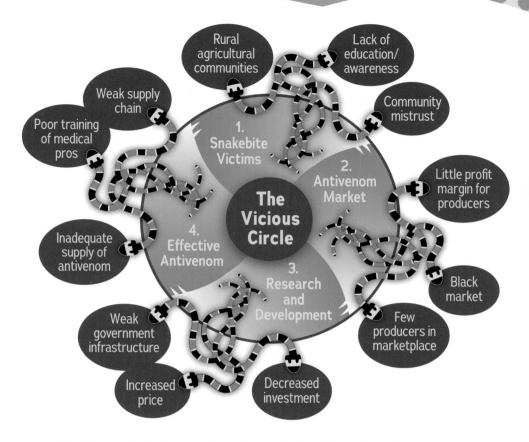

The Vicious Circle is created by a host of cultural, social, and economic forces. Each element (numbers 1 to 4) has many factors that contribute to preventing antivenom from reaching communities. The result is the never-ending Vicious Circle.

venomous snakes are abundant. Harvest season typically occurs during times of the year when snakes are most active, resulting in a spike of venomous snakebites. Some hospitals in Nigeria, for example, have reported that during harvest season, snakebite victims can occupy nearly every available bed.

Next, effective medicines such as antivenom can be extremely expensive to produce. One vial of antivenom can cost thousands of dollars, and snakebite patients often require more than one vial.

The cost for rural hospitals with small budgets is so high that the hospitals usually don't keep supplies of antivenom in stock. Even the most inexpensive antivenoms can cause serious financial hardship for an individual bitten by a snake. If the individual doesn't have medical insurance, the choice might be between rejecting antivenom treatment—which might result in death—or purchasing the antivenom, which might lead to financial ruin. The medicine is expensive to produce, and antivenom manufacturers don't always make much profit from it, so they do not produce large amounts of it. As a result, supplies of antivenom remain low in many parts of the world. Only a small handful of manufacturers provide antivenom to the entire African continent.

The final component is the lack of trust between medical workers and the communities in need. The rural communities in Africa, Asia, and India most affected by snakebites are often very traditional and sometimes distrust modern medicine as well as foreign medical workers. Medical workers in Africa and Asia who are fighting the Vicious Circle are combating generations of mistrust between traditional communities and modern medicine. Thanks to decades of ineffective and expensive antivenom, as well as sometimes poorly trained medical workers, large swaths of populations affected by snakebites believe going to the hospital means spending a lot of money on a treatment that might not work.

TRADITIONAL HEALING

People in these communities often prefer local healers and traditional methods of healing. For example, in rural areas of sub-Saharan Africa, up to 80 percent of snakebite victims may first seek the help of traditional healers in their own communities. These healers use a variety of methods. They may apply a tourniquet that cuts off the flow of blood to slow the spread of the snake venom, or they may use local herbs and medicines that are ultimately ineffective. One method even uses parts of cremated snakes, ground down to a powder and rubbed into the site of the bite.

As Boyer explains, "If the people don't have that trust [of modern medicine] and don't go in to seek help—then you've just wasted a lot of money on [providing] an expensive product, and people will lose faith." In other words, if snakebite patients don't seek help in modern hospitals, the vials of antivenom sit unused on shelves. Then hospitals do not reorder the medicine, and manufacturers do not receive profits from antivenom products, and the Vicious Circle keeps turning. Boyer says, "Trust has to build. . . . We need for people to hear there is a reliable cure if you get to the hospital fast. As more patients go in and more doctors treat more patients, more outcomes will be good."

Defeating the Vicious Circle will require help from people in many different fields, from medical and government workers to economists and educators. But the problem can be reversed. It begins with understanding.

CHAPTER 2
A WORLD OF VENOMOUS SNAKES

Venomous snakes are all around us. They roam the deciduous (leaf-shedding) forests of New England and the lowland marshes of Florida. They live in the prairies of Canada, the deserts of Mexico, the plains of Africa, and the outback of Australia. Venomous snakes live on every continent on Earth except for the Arctic and Antarctica.

Snakes are reptiles, a class of animals that includes alligators and lizards, turtles and tortoises. Reptiles have scales to protect them from the often harsh environments in which they thrive. They are cold-blooded—they rely on heat sources such as the sun to maintain their body temperature. Of the three thousand or so snake species found worldwide, about six hundred are venomous.

Many species of coral snake are found around the world. This Central American coral snake (*Micrurus nigrocinctus*) lives in the forests of countries such as Mexico, Nicaragua, Honduras, and Panama.

Some venomous snakes live in trees, while others live belowground. Some even live at sea. Venomous snakes can be timid and shy, seen by only the most daring scientists exploring remote corners of Earth. Depending on where you live, others might be right outside your door, beneath a dark shrub, waiting and watching for prey.

COEXISTENCE

Humans have a long and complicated relationship with snakes. Throughout history, these animals have been celebrated and feared, revered as icons, and killed for sport. The ancient Egyptians and Greeks, for example, used snake imagery widely in art and architecture, and snakes figured prominently in their myths and legends. In Hinduism, a major religion in India, the snake can represent both power and desire. In the biblical book of Genesis, an interaction with a devious serpent leads to the banishment of Adam and Eve—the world's first man and woman—from the Garden of Eden.

American Indians such as the Hopi, who have lived in the southwestern United States for centuries, revere the rattlesnakes that roam the desert. The Hopi believe that rattlesnakes are the guardians of water, a precious resource in the desert Southwest. Well into the twentieth century, they held secret rituals that lasted for days, in which participants danced while holding snakes in their mouths. Meanwhile, some modern Christian sects in rural areas of the southern United States call for people to handle deadly venomous snakes to demonstrate their faith in the Holy Spirit. In other parts of the United States, snakes are killed for sport. In Texas snake hunters round up the reptiles by the thousands and kill them in annual celebrations known as rattlesnake roundups.

Sweetwater, Texas, holds an annual rattlesnake roundup where thousands of rattlesnakes are captured and killed. Supporters of this controversial event say it helps control the population of dangerous snakes. Opponents say the ritual is an unnecessary killing of an important part of an ecosystem. As snake handlers prepare to weigh the two thousand live snakes in this pit, they use hooks to move the snakes to keep them from suffocating.

Snakes don't want to frighten people. Like all wildlife, they just want to be left alone. Yet as the human population on Earth grows beyond 7.6 billion and as cities and towns expand, humans have encroached on their lands with backyards, hiking trails, and rambunctious dogs. We live in their world. We always have. Snakes aren't going anywhere anytime soon, and that's a good thing. After all, we need snakes—even the venomous ones. Like other predators, snakes play a critical role in controlling populations of mice, rats, and other rodents.

LIVING WITH SNAKES

Some scientists think that our human fear of snakes can be traced back to the dawn of human evolution. Humans are primates—the group of mammals that includes lemurs, monkeys, gorillas, and chimpanzees. The earliest primates were small, timid creatures that lived in trees. Their eyes were closer to the sides of the skull than to the front, so they didn't have good depth perception—the ability to comprehend distance relative to the body. Instead, these early primates relied mostly on touch and smell to collect resources and live in their environments. Early primates were prey for large and deadly animals, including snakes, so they were always on the watch for these reptiles.

Over millions of years, the primates that learned to avoid the dangers of snakes and other threats survived to pass on their traits to their offspring. This process is known as natural selection. Individuals that are able to adapt to changing environments survive and pass along their deoxyribonucleic acid (DNA), or genetic information, to the next generation.

Eventually, the diets of our primate ancestors changed from plants to a more protein-based meat diet. With this change in diet, over time, the primate brain grew larger and developed increased functionality. In other words, primates became smarter. In addition, their eyes eventually moved toward the front of the skull, which allowed for greater depth perception. By about thirty-four million years ago, primates were relying more on the senses of vision and hearing than touch and smell. With improved vision and intelligence, these early primates were able to detect threats, including snakes, from a distance—before they got too close. Our earliest ancestors became wary of the constant threats surrounding them in the environment. They learned how to survive.

Modern humans are well-equipped biologically to avoid snakes, but we still carry our age-old fear of slithering serpents, be they large or small, dangerous or harmless. Studies have shown that in a laboratory, even modern-day primates such as chimpanzees demonstrate defensive reactions when shown simple images of snakes. Meanwhile, in the wild, monkeys, chimps, and many other social primates can respond to snakes with mobbing, a defensive strategy in which a group of animals surrounds the threat in an attempt to scare it off. There's even evidence that humans have inherited a natural ability to sense when snakes are near before we even see them. We've come a long way since our earliest evolutionary ancestors first came down from the treetops. Yet our inherent fear of snakes remains with us.

ALL IN THE (VENOMOUS) FAMILY

When it comes to venomous snakes, it all started about 170 million years ago. Venom first appeared in an ancient group of cold-blooded animals known as *Toxicofera*. Over time, this group evolved and diversified to walk, crawl, swim, and slither. Eventually *Toxicofera* grew to include modern-day venomous lizards, iguanas, and snakes. They live in nearly every biome (community of distinct plants and animals in a particular environment) on Earth.

Scientists have classified about 680 species of snakes worldwide as venomous. Deadly snakes mostly are grouped into two large families: Viperidae and Elapidae. Viperidae is the family of venomous snakes known as vipers. These snakes are found around the globe, from the

THE NAME GAME

Earth is full of billions of different kinds of living things, or organisms. Throughout history, to make it easier to study and talk about these living things, scientists have developed ways to organize and categorize organisms. The science of naming, describing, and classifying living things is taxonomy. Scientists study the behavior, anatomy, and other characteristics of living things to separate them into groups of related creatures. This type of classification also helps with understanding evolutionary relationships. The broadest category of living things is the Domain. There are three domains: Archaea, Bacteria, and Eukarya. From there, organisms are broken down into narrower and narrower categories: Kingdom, Phylum, Class, Order, Family, Genus, and Species. Organisms of the same species are able to mate and produce viable offspring.

In the eighteenth century, a Swedish botanist named Carl Linnaeus came up with a consistent and efficient system for naming individual organisms. He settled on Latin as the main language of taxonomy. Together a specific genus and species name refers to one organism. For example, the scientific name for the copperhead snake is *Agkistrodon contortrix.* The two-word taxonomic naming system is known as binomial nomenclature. Although few people speak or use the language, Latin acts as a universal language of science.

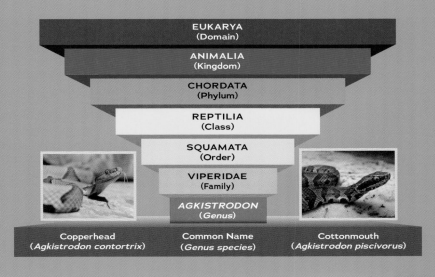

| EUKARYA (Domain) |
| ANIMALIA (Kingdom) |
| CHORDATA (Phylum) |
| REPTILIA (Class) |
| SQUAMATA (Order) |
| VIPERIDAE (Family) |
| *AGKISTRODON* (*Genus*) |

| Copperhead (*Agkistrodon contortrix*) | Common Name (*Genus species*) | Cottonmouth (*Agkistrodon piscivorus*) |

Middle East and Asia to the Americas. Many Viperidae species are known as pit vipers. They are named for sensory organs known as sensory pits. These small openings are on the front of the snake's head between the nostrils and the eyes. These sensory organs can detect heat. This helps snakes sense the body heat of their prey, mostly small, warm-blooded animals such as rats and other rodents. Once vipers detect the prey, they extend their forked tongues out of their mouths to pick up tiny scent molecules in the air. This allows the snake to "smell" the surrounding air, which includes the scent of the prey animal, and to close in on the prey.

In North America, the copperhead (*Agkistrodon contortrix*) and cottonmouth (*Agkistrodon piscivorus*) are two types of common pit vipers. Usually they live in wetland habitats throughout the eastern United States, from the Louisiana lowlands to the New Hampshire highlands. The most notorious of all pit vipers are rattlesnakes. About thirty-seven species of rattlesnakes live in North America, mostly in the southwestern deserts of the United States and Mexico. These areas are the snakes' ancestral home, where venomous vipers first appeared some

A snake's sensory pits, located between the nostrils and the eyes, can detect the body heat of other animals up to 3.3 feet (1 m) away. The snake in this photo is a copperhead.

twelve million years ago. In the arid Southwest, few other kinds of predators have been able to survive for as long as the rattlesnake.

ELAPIDS

Elapids—snakes of the family Elapidae—have earned legendary status. They are responsible for thousands of human deaths and countless injuries each year, mostly in rural, agricultural areas of Africa and Southeast Asia. The most infamous members of the Elapidae family—death adders, mambas, and cobras—are known for their size, speed, aggressive nature, and potent venom.

Elapids are a very widespread and diverse family of snakes. Almost all species are found in tropical and subtropical environments, from the lush forests of Southeast Asia to the dense jungles of Africa. Some elapids even live in the oceans. Sea snakes have a unique striped pattern and a flat, oarlike tail that propels them through the water. Almost all species of sea snakes live in the waters of Australia and the South Pacific Ocean. In recent years, researchers discovered the pelagic (open ocean) sea snake (*Pelamis platurus*) off the shores of Hawaii, in the North Pacific Ocean.

In the Americas, elapid snakes include a dozen or so species of coral snakes. Generally very timid, coral snakes rarely bite people, but their venom is extremely powerful. A few species of coral snakes live in the United States in habitats from the coastal plains of North Carolina to the vast grasslands of Arizona. Many more coral snake species live in Central and South America. Most of them are colorfully banded black, red, and yellow. The bright colors mean "don't touch." It's a natural warning system that has been a very successful evolutionary feature. In fact, several harmless, nonvenomous species such as the scarlet king snake (*Lampropeltis elasoides*) have evolved similar patterns to keep predators away.

Compared to their viper cousins, elapids are much more diverse in size and shape. Some elapid species, such as the notorious death adders

There are many different species of cobra, recognizable by the hood near their heads. When threatened, cobras extend their hoods, raise their upper bodies, and hiss. Humans bitten by a cobra may stop breathing within thirty minutes of the bite.

of Australia, are short and stocky. Just one look and you know a death adder is dangerous. (And a pretty cool name sure helps!) Meanwhile, other species of elapids can be enormous. Many elapid snakes regularly grow to 8 or 10 feet (2.4 or 3 m) long. The king cobra (*Ophiophagus hannah*), for example, is the world's longest venomous snake, stretching up to 18 feet (5.6 m) long!

WEAPONS AND STRATEGIES

At the Arizona-Sonora Desert Museum, west of Tucson, Arizona, venomous snakes surround herpetologist Stephane Poulin. (Herpetologists study reptiles and amphibians.) One part of his office is lined with small tanks housing about two dozen different species of venomous snakes, including rattlesnakes, that are found in the desert

Southwest. Just opening the door and entering the room sets off a chorus of chilling rattles.

Using a pair of long tools called snake hooks, Poulin reaches into a tank and gently collects a rattlesnake, balancing the slithering serpent between the two hooks. Poulin handles rattlesnakes with the same skill and ease other people might display when typing on a keyboard or tying a shoe. It's just another day at the office for him.

"Venom is a tool," he explains as the snake glides from hook to hook. "If you look at predators and prey, any time you're going to have to grab onto a prey, it's going to be dangerous. And being a predator is really tough. Finding ways to dispatch [kill] prey very quickly is in your advantage."

For rattlers, their success as a predator comes from many key attributes. Rattlesnakes use crypsis, or the art of camouflage. Most rattlesnakes have stripes and other patterns that help them blend or virtually vanish into their surroundings. For a rattlesnake, crypsis is the first line of defense against any hungry predator such as a coyote or hawk.

Stephane Poulin, a herpetologist at the Arizona-Sonora Desert Museum in Tucson, Arizona, uses snake hooks to handle a venomous snake in his office.

Camouflage also allows the snake to stay hidden away from its prey. Venomous snakes often ambush their prey. They lie hidden and motionless, waiting patiently until a prey animal wanders too close. Then . . . *Wham!* The snake strikes.

Rattlers and other venomous snakes have evolved a sophisticated venom delivery system called the venom apparatus. Each snake has a pair of venom glands, one on each side of the head near the base of the skull. The venom glands are modified salivary glands. They produce and store the snake's deadly venom until it is used in a bite. Attached to each gland are small ducts, or tubes, which deliver venom to the snake's fangs. Rattlesnakes and some other venomous snakes have hypodermic fangs. They are hollow, like a needle at the doctor's office. But instead of delivering healing medicine, these fangs deliver a potent dose of venom.

When not in use, the fangs lie flat along the roof of the snake's mouth. But during a strike—that split second when a snake bites its

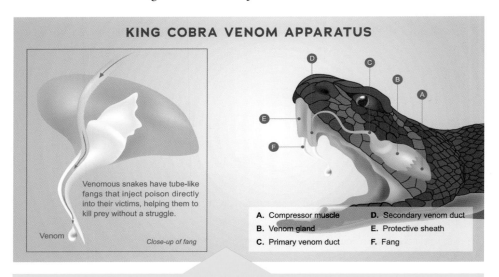

KING COBRA VENOM APPARATUS

Venomous snakes have tube-like fangs that inject poison directly into their victims, helping them to kill prey without a struggle.

Venom

Close-up of fang

A. Compressor muscle
B. Venom gland
C. Primary venom duct
D. Secondary venom duct
E. Protective sheath
F. Fang

King cobras are elapids. Their compressor muscles are weaker than those of vipers, so their venom delivery is less accurate. Elapid fangs are also different from those of vipers. Vipers have hinged fangs that fold against the top of the mouth when not in use and flare forward when the snake strikes. Elapid fangs are fixed in place.

victim—the fangs flick open like a switchblade knife. When the snake's spring-loaded body strikes, its mouth snaps open almost 180 degrees. The sharp fangs flare out, and the snake buries its teeth into the skin of its prey. Muscles contract to force venom out of the venom glands, and it shoots through the ducts, out the fangs, and into the victim. Vipers have well-developed muscles around their venom glands. They can quickly and accurately deliver venom to their prey.

Unlike rattlers, most elapids have fixed fangs that remain in position in the upper jaw. Elapids also have weaker muscles around the venom glands. When they bite a victim, the glands deliver the venom more slowly and less accurately than vipers do. Some elapids grab hold of their dinner and slowly release the venom into their victim, appearing to chew on it until the prey animal is helpless.

If the sheer size and aggressiveness of these snakes wasn't terrifying enough, some elapid species defend themselves by spitting venom! Spitting cobras live in parts of Africa and Southeast Asia. They have modified hollow fangs that allow them to spray deadly venom. They usually aim for the eyes of a potential threat. If on target, the venom will cause severe pain and even permanent blindness.

ENERGETICS

Nature's most basic law is eat or be eaten. For a venomous snake, the more effective its venom, the better chance the snake has of eating that day. Powerful venom allows the snake to be more efficient as a hunter. And managing this supply of venom is key to survival.

All animals, whether prey or predator, have a certain amount of energy they can use for eating, sleeping, and surviving. This is called energetics. If a bobcat spends a lot of time and energy chasing down a desert cottontail rabbit, that effort had better pay off in a meal. If that energy expenditure is unsuccessful—no rabbit—the bobcat will have to go without a meal and without as much energy for the next hunt. Being a successful hunter usually means being an efficient hunter.

THE RATTLE

The most distinct feature of the rattlesnake is its warning rattle. When threatened, the snake vibrates its tail and the rattle releases an unmistakable and chilling sound. It's a sound you only have to hear once. This is the snake's way of saying, "Back off!"

The rattle is actually a series of hollow tubelike structures at the end of the snake's tail. They are made of keratin, the same substance that makes up human hair and fingernails. The snake vibrates its tail back and forth, and the hollow segments bounce off one another to produce that wicked sound.

Contrary to popular belief, rattlesnakes are not aggressive animals. They spend much of their day basking in the sun or hiding, waiting for a meal to pass by. They only bite as a last resort when they feel threatened or when a prey animal is within reach. The same is true of their rattle. A rattlesnake would much rather stay hidden away and let a person walk by. It will sound its alarm only when it has no other options left.

"If I'm a predator, the moment that you rattle is the moment you rang the dinner bell. Now I know where you are," Poulin says. "Snakes are part of the food chain, too. So staying invisible is the best thing for them to do."

Rattlesnakes shed their skin, sometimes several times a year. Each time they shed, the tubelike rattle at the end of the tail gains another segment. This rattlesnake has six segments in its rattle.

Reptiles have a very different energetics equation than mammals do. All reptiles are ectothermic (cold blooded). A lizard or snake basking in the sun is soaking in those warm rays to raise its body temperature. Increased body temperature helps fuel the animal's metabolism. This complex system of internal chemical reactions helps the animal digest food and absorb nutrients that will be turned into energy. In venomous snakes, metabolism also helps produce venom.

Warm-blooded mammals need to eat regularly to maintain their metabolisms and ensure their bodies function properly. Cold-blooded reptiles, however, can go for long stretches of time without refueling with a meal. They can meet their yearly energy budget with just a few large meals. This rule of energetics helps explain why so many reptiles live in arid deserts where food and water are scarce. They simply don't need to eat as much as warm-blooded animals do.

Energetics may also explain why venomous snakes don't always deliver venom to their victims. Up to 40 percent of their bites do not contain venom. These are known as dry bites. Snakes have a very good reason for using a dry bite. To the snake, venom is very costly to make. To produce the toxic component of venom from their venom glands, the snake needs to greatly increase its metabolic rate—the amount of energy needed to maintain normal bodily functions. Following a venomous bite, a rattlesnake might increase its metabolic rate by up to 11 percent for three days to replace its venom.

So venomous snakes are careful with what they do with their venom. Dry bites can successfully deter a threat while conserving venom and energy. Often it is inefficient to use venom on a mountain lion or elephant (or human) when the snake just wants to scare away the threat. A dry bite will do just fine. If a snake is going to use venom, it will most likely use it on smaller prey. A venomous bite in that scenario is more likely to result in a meal. The energy tradeoff is worth it. In a snake's world, when you need to eat, you'd better make it count.

CHAPTER 3
A TOXIC BREW

Venomous animals come in all shapes and sizes and are in nearly every phylum of the animal kingdom. They include venomous insects, spiders, jellyfish, fish, reptiles, and amphibians. There are even a few venomous mammals. The duck-billed platypus of Australia is one example. Male platypuses have sharp spurs hidden beneath the thick fur in their hind legs. These venomous spurs can deliver a lot of pain with just a little prick. To date, scientists have not discovered a single venomous bird, however, living or extinct.

The number of venomous species roaming Earth at any given moment can be mind-blowing. In Cnidarians alone (a phylum of animals that includes jellyfish, coral, and sea anemones), more than nine thousand species are considered venomous. But the group of animals with the most venomous species are the arthropods. This phylum of invertebrate animals

The Japanese sea nettle (*Chrysaora pacifica*) is one of Earth's many venomous animals. It has stinging tentacles, which it uses for gathering prey animals such as small fish. The tentacles work independently of one another, so the sea nettle is constantly feeding.

(those without internal skeletons) includes spiders, scorpions, and insects such as bees and wasps. With more than one million species of arthropods worldwide, scientists don't even know how many of them are venomous!

BY ANY OTHER NAME

Venom is a biological chemical used for defense or for the capture of food. It contains molecules that disrupt a prey's normal biological processes. These molecules are toxins, and they are the active ingredient in venom.

All successful predators have evolved physical traits that allow them to be effective in the hunt for food. They rely on sharp claws or teeth, speed, or strength to take down their prey. But some predators, like snakes, don't have claws or overpowering strength to help them catch food. Instead, they use venom. Think about it: Say you're a venomous

THE WORLD'S DEADLIEST ANIMAL

We generally think of venomous animals as having powerful, if not deadly, toxic venom. But venom can come in many different forms, and not all venoms are toxic to all animals. Take the typical mosquito. The annoying insect of the family Culicidae—with about three thousand species—is perhaps the world's deadliest venomous animal.

Mosquitoes have venomous chemicals in their saliva, which they use for feeding. Some chemicals in the saliva numb the area of the bite so the victim is unaware of the pesky mosquito stabbing at the skin to get to the precious bloody meal below. Another chemical in the saliva prevents the blood from clotting. This keeps the blood flowing for a delicious meal for the mosquito.

Because mosquitoes can transfer tiny portions of blood from one individual to another while feeding, mosquitoes are good at spreading disease. Known as vectors, mosquitoes are responsible for spreading many deadly blood-borne illnesses such as malaria, yellow fever, and dengue fever.

As they feed, mosquitoes can spread deadly diseases such as Zika virus, chikungunya virus, dengue fever, and malaria. Because of their ability to spread disease, mosquitoes are some of the deadliest animals in the world.

Mosquito-spread diseases are responsible for killing hundreds of thousands (if not millions) of people each year. If you combined all the deaths from other venomous organisms, it wouldn't even be a fraction of the death toll racked up by mosquitoes. A mosquito's venomous bite does not directly harm or kill its victim, but its venom is still deadly.

predator such as a jellyfish or snake. You don't have legs to run down prey. You don't have arms or sharp claws to catch and hold an animal that is frantically kicking and squirming to get away. And you certainly don't have a set of strong teeth to tear and grind flesh so you can eat. But with venom, snakes and other venomous animals can overcome these evolutionary shortcomings. A venomous jellyfish can sting its prey, quickly immobilizing it. Then the jellyfish uses its long, flowing tentacles to latch on to the motionless prey and drag it into the jelly body for consumption.

This same strategy works for a venomous snake hunting a mouse. After the snake bites the mouse, the rodent may scramble away. But soon the snake's venom takes effect and shuts down the mouse's body systems. Patiently, the snake follows the mouse's scent. When it gets to the paralyzed mouse, the snake unhinges its jaw and slowly swallows the animal whole. Although a snake's fangs are sharp and deadly, these

The prongs of a snake's forked tongue fit into an organ in the roof of the mouth that sends sensory messages to the snake's brain to interpret scents.

VENOMOUS OR POISONOUS?

Although the terms *venomous* and *poisonous* are often used interchangeably, they are actually very different. Poisons and venoms both contain harmful toxins, but the way the toxins are delivered defines whether an animal is venomous or poisonous.

Poisonous plants and animals deliver toxins through absorption or ingestion by another creature. The poison is used strictly for defense. For example, poison ivy and poison oak are two toxic plants from the genus *Toxicodendron* that grow throughout much of the United States. Each possesses toxic oil that can cause serious allergic reactions, such as blisters and skin lesions, when it touches the skin. Animals such as poison dart frogs of South America have skin glands that contain powerful toxins. If any predator tried to eat one of these frogs, it would surely be its last meal. Toxins in the oil of poison ivy or the skin of dart frogs prevents them from being eaten by other animals.

Poison dart frogs do not produce their own toxins. Instead, scientists think the toxins come from the insects these frogs eat.

These species are poisonous because their toxins are used passively—the plant or animal doesn't take action to poison an enemy. The enemy touches or ingests the poison and is harmed.

To qualify as venomous, an animal must have an active means of delivering the toxins through a specific action by the venomous animal. The stinging tentacles of a jellyfish are one example. Within each of the jelly's tentacles are hundreds of structures called nematocysts, which work like tiny toxic harpoons. When triggered by unsuspecting passing prey, a spring-loaded barb bursts from the nematocyst, piercing the prey's skin to deliver a paralyzing toxin. The stunned fish is helpless as the jelly's long tentacles ensnare its prey. This act of delivering venom—through a sting or bite or some other weapon—is called envenomation.

teeth are delicate and are not very helpful when it comes to chewing food. So venom's deadly ingredients provide snakes with a shortcut. As the snake swallows the mouse, it releases the toxic venom. It liquefies the mouse, turning it into a tasty rodent smoothie that the snake can easily digest.

PICK YOUR POISON

Most organisms have a natural ability to fight toxins in low doses. They do this with the help of a healthy immune system. But these defenses are no match for snake venom. Venom overwhelms the immune system and the body's ability to fight the invading toxins. Venom is difficult to fight because so many different types of venom exist. Each species of venomous snake produces a specific type of venom, mixing different combinations of toxins into a deadly cocktail. Just one snake can possess up to one dozen different types of toxins!

These toxins attack different parts of the body. Necrotoxins destroy blood cells, while nephrotoxins target the kidneys. Myotoxins attack muscles, and cardiotoxins cause the heart to stop beating. Most snake venoms, however, fall into two general categories: hemotoxins or neurotoxins. Hemotoxins attack blood or tissues in skin and organs, either killing important tissues or causing massive bleeding. (The root *hemo-* is Latin for "blood.") Neurotoxins, meanwhile, go after the nervous system, causing bodily functions to stop working properly. The nervous system is the body's communication center, transferring information from the sensory organs such as the nose, eyes, and ears to the brain and muscles and everything else in between. Neurotransmitters are the chemical links between nerve cells that transfer information from nerve cell to nerve cell.

The toxins in venom are made up of large, complex molecules called proteins, which include carbon, oxygen, nitrogen, and hydrogen. Proteins are versatile and have many functions. Some proteins—called enzymes—can kick-start chemical reactions that help our bodies function properly.

THE IMMUNE SYSTEM

In mammals the immune system is a highly complex network of cells, tissues, and organs that protect the body from foreign invaders known as pathogens. These pathogens, or germs, are foreign cells that enter the body, usually through eating or breathing. The pathogens contain proteins called antigens that are unique to that pathogen. Some pathogens, such as plant pollen or cat hair, trigger mild allergic reactions such as sneezing or a skin rash. These mild reactions are simply signs that your immune system is fighting for you, trying to expel the annoying but mostly harmless pathogen.

Other pathogens cause great harm. These pathogens include bacteria, the microorganisms that cause terrible illnesses such as pneumonia or tuberculosis, and viruses, which lead to dangerous diseases such as influenza or Ebola. Viruses infect the body by invading cells and producing more viruses.

When pathogens enter the body, the immune system identifies, attacks, and destroys the harmful pathogens before they can reproduce and cause too much damage. The soldiers in this never-ending battle are a variety of cells produced by the body's lymphatic system, which helps rid the body of toxins. Some of the most important cells are white blood cells known as T cells and B cells. When these cells identify the antigens, the B cells produce antibodies, proteins that lock onto the antigen and prevent them from doing harm. Then the T cells, along with other immune cells, go to work to attack and destroy the pathogens. The antibodies stay in the body, ready to attack the pathogens if they ever return. Because of these antibodies, the body has become immune to this particular disease.

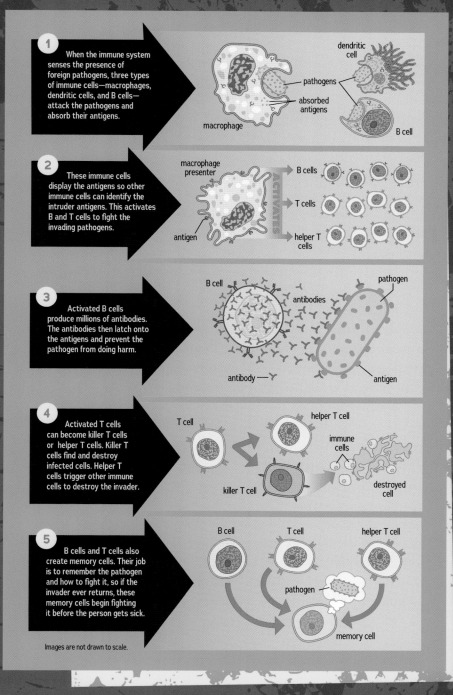

1 When the immune system senses the presence of foreign pathogens, three types of immune cells—macrophages, dendritic cells, and B cells—attack the pathogens and absorb their antigens.

dendritic cell

pathogens

absorbed antigens

macrophage

B cell

2 These immune cells display the antigens so other immune cells can identify the intruder antigens. This activates B and T cells to fight the invading pathogens.

macrophage presenter

ACTIVATES

B cells

T cells

helper T cells

antigen

3 Activated B cells produce millions of antibodies. The antibodies then latch onto the antigens and prevent the pathogen from doing harm.

B cell

antibodies

pathogen

antibody

antigen

4 Activated T cells can become killer T cells or helper T cells. Killer T cells find and destroy infected cells. Helper T cells trigger other immune cells to destroy the invader.

T cell

helper T cell

immune cells

killer T cell

destroyed cell

5 B cells and T cells also create memory cells. Their job is to remember the pathogen and how to fight it, so if the invader ever returns, these memory cells begin fighting it before the person gets sick.

B cell

T cell

helper T cell

pathogen

memory cell

Images are not drawn to scale.

Muscle proteins such as actin and myosin help muscles contract and relax. Other proteins help transport oxygen in blood and muscles. Still other proteins, including keratin and collagen, provide structure for hair and nails.

While most proteins help keep us healthy, some proteins can have horrible effects. The proteins in hemotoxins target red blood cells. These cells carry oxygen all around an animal's body, delivering life-giving oxygen molecules to tissues and organs. The proteins in hemotoxins destroy the walls of red blood cells so they can no longer function as container units that deliver the precious oxygen molecules. Unable to carry oxygen, tissue and organs starve and begin to die.

Other hemotoxins destroy the clotting mechanisms in blood. A blood clot is critical for slowing or stopping bleeding. For example, when you cut yourself, blood will drip out of the open wound. Then blood cells called platelets bind together at the site of the injury to form a gooey mass. What's left behind is a scab, which protects the wound while your skin mends itself. Without the ability to clot and stop the flow of blood, an animal will bleed to death.

Neurotoxins attack the nervous system. The proteins in neurotoxins specifically attack neurotransmitters and disrupt the communication links throughout the nervous system. When the line of communication within the nervous system breaks down, things can go wrong very quickly. Nerves can trigger muscles into uncontrollable spastic fits. Or nerves can shut down, causing the muscles to constrict until they can no longer function. Paralysis sets in, leaving prey helpless. Eventually the envenomated prey will be unable to breath and will die by suffocation.

Most venom possesses different types of toxins all mixed together. Hemotoxic venoms might have a small dose of neurotoxins as well as a dash of necrotoxin. Another venom might have equal doses of neurotoxins, necrotoxins, and a pinch of cardiotoxins. The combinations of venoms make fighting venom so difficult.

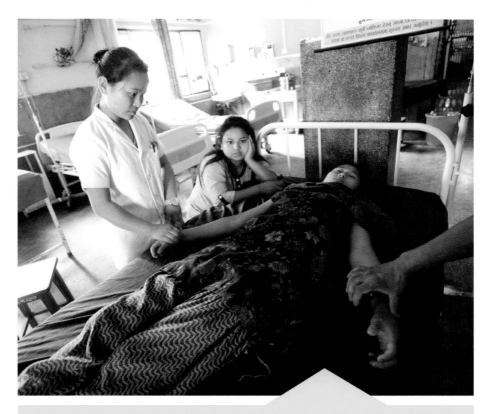

A nurse checks on a fifteen-year-old snakebite patient at Teku hospital in Kathmandu, Nepal. Nepal is home to seventeen species of venomous snakes. Many of them have neurotoxic venom that causes paralysis to the nervous system and respiratory system. During monsoon season (a period of heavy rains) each year, Teku hospital sees as many as twenty snakebite patients each day.

Prey have only a small chance of fighting off the deadly effects of venom. If the hemotoxin doesn't kill or immobilize the prey, the neurotoxin in the mix will. The complexity of venom makes it effective over time as an evolutionary benefit. It ensures that venomous animals stay one step ahead of prey or threats in an eat-or-be-eaten world. But every once in a while, some animals catch up to venomous snakes.

MIRROR, MIRROR ON THE WALL, WHO'S THE DEADLIEST OF THEM ALL?

With the seemingly endless number of venomous creatures worldwide, which is the most deadly? A rattlesnake? A spider? A duck-billed platypus? The answer depends on how you ask the question.

Scientists generally categorize venom on a scale of potency, or the strength of the toxins. This scale is known as LD_{50}. *LD* stands for "lethal dose," while 50 means "50 percent of lab mice." So LD_{50} represents the amount of venom that will kill 50 percent of mice in a laboratory. The lower the LD_{50} value, the more potent the venom. To find the animal with the lowest LD_{50} and therefore the most potent venom, head to the South Pacific Ocean. Just don't touch anything! There you will find the geographer cone snail (*Conus geographus*), known to have the most powerful of all venoms. It can kill a grown human within minutes.

The geographer cone snail has the most potent venom of any animal on Earth. It delivers venom through a harpoonlike tooth in its proboscis, which sticks out from the shell near the siphon.

In the world of snakes, the most venomous—with the lowest LD_{50}—are two types of elapid snakes found in Australia: the inland taipan (*Oxyuranus microlepidotus)* and the coastal taipan (*Oxyuranus scutellatus*). In North America, the Mojave rattlesnake (*Crotalus scutulatus*) of the desert Southwest packs the most punch. While deadly, these snakes rarely encounter humans.

But when we want to know which snake is the deadliest, we usually mean, "Which snake is deadliest to humans?" The answer to this question is the Big Four of India: the Indian cobra (*Naja naja*), the common krait (*Bungarus caeruleus*), the Russell's viper (*Daboia russelii*), and the saw-scaled viper (*Echis carinatus*). This group of elapids and vipers kills tens of thousands of humans each year. These four species are the deadliest not because their venoms are more powerful than that of other species but because these venomous snakes live close to humans. They have adapted to living near rural villages and coexisting with humans. It's a simple equation: more human interaction with venomous snakes leads to more venomous bites. And more venomous bites cause more human deaths.

PREDATOR OR PREY?

In any ecosystem, the predator-prey relationship is a delicate balance between competing animals. A tip either way can result in drastic changes to populations of either competitor. A predator that overhunts its prey will soon run out of food. And prey that can't outsmart or outrun a predator will soon become extinct. Since they have such an intimate relationship, many predators and prey coevolve—they evolve alongside one another, each species struggling to survive and create the next generation. Successful predators and prey are those that have strategies, defenses, and weapons that ensure survival. Sometimes the predator wins. Other times the prey wins. Even deadly venomous snakes must follow the basic rules of this predator-prey relationship.

Over time, say thousands of years, prey can develop immunity, or the natural ability to fight the effects of venom. Prey that has developed immunity to venom is no longer prey for venomous creatures. For example, in North America, the common king snake (*Lampropeltis getula*) is not vulnerable to the deadly effects of rattlesnake venom, which is mostly hemotoxic. As a result, the king snake is one of the few animals that actively prey on rattlesnakes.

Meanwhile, the gray mongoose (*Herpestes edwardsii*) of India is immune to the highly venomous cobra snakes that live in the region. (Having extremely dense fur and thick skin to deflect a cobra bite helps too.) Immunity to cobra venom not only helps the mongoose survive, but it can also result in a hearty meal. A freshly killed cobra could feed a whole mongoose family.

How are the king snake and mongoose able to resist venom? In these animals, when the immune system identifies an invading venom toxin after a bite, the body releases protein inhibitors. These proteins attach themselves to the attacking venom molecules. The toxin is then unable to bind to its target, such as a red blood cell, and cannot destroy that cell. The invading toxin has become harmless.

Indian gray mongooses eat a range of deadly snakes. The mongoose is immune to snake venom, and it can also fight venomous snakes. The mongoose provokes the snake until the snake tires. Then the mongoose goes in for the kill, biting the snake and cracking its skull.

Not every animal can fight off powerful venom toxins in this way. If you're not a mongoose or a king snake, a venomous snakebite can be real trouble. But science has figured out how to fight back. Researchers have harnessed the power of immunity and repackaged it as an effective medicine to combat deadly venom. It's a defense called antivenom.

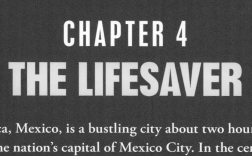

CHAPTER 4
THE LIFESAVER

Cuernavaca, Mexico, is a bustling city about two hours south of the nation's capital of Mexico City. In the center of Cuernavaca sits Barranca de Chapultepec, a zoo and park filled with waterfalls and towering Montezuma cypress trees. They display the lush, semitropical environment of the region.

At the zoo's herpetarium—the reptile and amphibian collection—it is venom extraction day. Edgar and Melisa, two students from the Universidad Nacional Autónoma de México (National Autonomous University of Mexico, or UNAM), are setting up equipment. Small glass aquariums, each containing a venomous serpent from a different region of the world, surround them. Among these snakes are a massive horned Gaboon viper from the rain forests of Africa, an 8-foot (2.4 m) spitting cobra from India, and a tropical rattlesnake from Mexico.

Fernando (*left*), the manager of the herpetarium at Barranca de Chapultepec, works with Edgar and Melisa, two students from the Universidad Nacional Autónoma de México. They carefully handle a spitting cobra as they prepare to collect its venom.

Edgar and Melisa have years of training in handling these snakes. Still, it takes a steady hand and serious concentration. Just one little slip, one small lapse in concentration, can result in a trip to the hospital.

Antivenom production begins at the herpetarium, and the first step is collecting venom from these dangerous snakes. Venomous snakes don't like being disturbed. And they especially don't like giving up their precious potion. But this work is important. Venom from these snakes will be used to produce antivenoms for Africa, Asia, and other parts of the world.

Soon Edgar and Melisa are ready to milk their first snake. Using long snake hooks, Edgar gently wrangles the spitting cobra from its glass cage. After some delicate maneuvering, he coaxes the slithering cobra into a long plastic tube. The tube is narrow enough so the snake cannot move, and only its head is exposed. Now they can handle the deadly cobra safely.

Melisa gently grabs the snake behind its head and places her fingers right over the cobra's venom glands. She gently guides the snake's head toward the collection jar, and the snake's mouth flares open to reveal its fangs. As the snake sinks its teeth into the film covering the mouth of the jar, Melisa gently massages the snake's cheeks, delicately squeezing the venom glands on each side. The flow of venom soon begins. A thick, yellow liquid oozes out of the snake's hollow fangs and drips down the inside of the glass jar, pooling at the bottom. Next, Edgar and Melisa delicately collect the precious venom and transfer it into small vials where it will be placed in cool storage before the venom embarks on the next stage of its epic journey to becoming lifesaving antivenom.

Melisa milks a snake by gently squeezing its venom glands to release the yellow venom that drips from the snake's fangs into the collection jar.

THE JOURNEY OF ANTIVENOM PRODUCTION

Edgar and Melisa are students of Dr. Alejandro Alagón, a professor at UNAM and a world leader in venom research. Students in his laboratory study all kinds of venoms from snakes, spiders, scorpions, and other venomous creatures. They examine the complex structures of venom molecules and their various toxins. By studying venoms at their most basic level, they can understand how to create antivenoms that are effective against a wide range of venoms. "We are generating basic knowledge of venoms," Alagón says. "And that knowledge immediately translates to applied knowledge [practical uses for that knowledge]."

Not all venoms are created equal. Out of the six hundred or so venomous snake species known worldwide, only about two hundred of these species are considered medically important. These highly venomous snake species cause many dangerous bites each year. While the United States hosts just a few medically important species, sub-Saharan Africa is home to dozens of these dangerous snake species. Creating antivenoms from these medically important species is critical to combating the snakebite crisis.

Dr. Alejandro Alagón, a professor at UNAM, works closely with Boyer to develop antivenoms that are used around the world. The collaboration between the two scientists and their teams is creating a wide range of antivenoms that are reliable and cost-effective.

IT'S IN THE BLOOD

The secret ingredient to antivenom is in blood, mostly from animals such as pigs, sheep, and horses. Mammal blood has solid parts and liquid parts. The solid parts are three types of blood cells. These include red blood cells that carry oxygen throughout the body and white blood cells that play a critical role in maintaining the immune system. Platelets, which cause clotting, are a third type of solid blood cell.

The liquid portion of blood is called plasma. It helps protect the delicate solid blood cells and is the fluid in which blood cells move freely throughout the body, getting quickly to the places they need to go. Plasma is mostly composed of water, but it is also made of several types of proteins known as antibodies. Like the protein inhibitors in mongooses and king snakes, antibodies render venom useless.

Lab workers produce antivenom using these powerful antibodies in mammal blood. It starts with hyperimmunization. During hyperimmunization, a worker will inject a series of small, harmless doses of venom into a horse or other large mammal over weeks or months. The animal's body goes to work fighting the venom. Gradually, as more venom is injected, the body increases its defenses against the venom. The animal's immune system will eventually produce enough antibodies to overwhelm the venom and make it useless. Once the animal's blood has produced a significant amount of antibodies, the blood can be collected to make antivenom.

COWBOYS AND ANTIVENOM

Just outside the small village of Agua Fria in the state of Puebla, Mexico, roosters announce that the day is beginning. The sun has yet to rise, and it is still too dark to see, but activity is well under way. A few voices in the distance give instructions, and an old gate creaks open. From somewhere in the darkness comes the gentle sound of hooves meandering into a corral. At first, just a few, then many more. As first light breaks, dozens of horses are wandering into the corral.

VACCINES AND ANTIVENOM

In 1796 an English doctor named Edward Jenner launched a medical revolution. People in many parts of the world were suffering outbreaks of smallpox. This virus was killing thousands of children each year in Europe alone. Meanwhile, in the rural, agricultural areas of England, a similar but far less deadly disease called cowpox was affecting local milkmaids, the young women who worked closely with cows and other livestock on farms. Doctors began to notice that women affected by the nuisance cowpox virus never contracted the deadly smallpox virus.

Jenner decided to perform a risky experiment. The doctor took a small amount of the cowpox virus and introduced it to a small child who was otherwise healthy. After a few days, Jenner exposed the child to the harmful smallpox virus. Jenner found that the boy did not contract the smallpox. The boy's immune system had learned to fight back against the virus. With this groundbreaking discovery, Jenner created the world's first vaccine.

Vaccines work by introducing a dead or otherwise harmless form of a virus or bacterium into the body. The vaccination triggers an immune response that destroys the virus or bacterium before it has a chance to infect cells, replicate, and spread inside the body. Later, if the virus or bacterium attacks the body again, T cells and B cells will remember the specific invader. These cells will produce antibodies that specifically target and destroy the invader.

In the United States, young people are regularly vaccinated against once-common diseases such as mumps, measles, and rubella. These diseases, which can be deadly, have been almost wiped out through widespread public vaccination programs. As for smallpox, the disease has all but vanished, thanks to vaccines.

Edward Jenner (1749–1823) was the first to vaccinate a patient against smallpox. This illustration shows an experiment in which he infected his infant son wth swinepox.

Horses feed at Ojo de Agua Ranch in Agua Fria, Mexico. These horses are a key part of producing the raw materials for antivenom.

It is breakfast time at the ranch. For some of the horses, it is also blood collection day.

This is the Ojo de Agua Ranch. It has been in Alagón's family for generations. Once it operated as a dairy farm, housing dozens of milk cows. These days, the ranch is home to more than 120 horses that play an important role in the production of antivenom. Each year, Alagón's horses help create more than twenty thousand vials of antivenom. The pharmaceutical company Inosan Biopharma will sell them in Europe and Africa.

The horses at the ranch regularly have their blood drawn. Their antibodies are the raw material for antivenom. The horses are well fed and cared for, spending most days lazily grazing in the ranch's rolling pastures. It's a good life for a horse. "The trick is you need to treat the horses well," Alagón says, giving away the secret behind his successful antivenom production. Managing more than a hundred horses requires many ranch hands and cowboys who constantly care for the horses—they clean, feed, and move the horses to and from the picturesque pastures in which they spend their days. "We have spoiled horses here at the ranch," Alagón says.

The horses are also here to work. About fifteen ranch hands and managers keep the horses on a strict schedule. Every few weeks, each horse receives a series of injections containing tiny, harmless doses of venom from snakes, scorpions, or another venomous source. During hyperimmunization, each horse's robust immune system goes to work fighting the introduced toxins. Over six months, each horse's immune system will produce a rich supply of antibodies.

Then it is time to collect blood from the horses. Ranch hands lead each horse into a small holding pen. There they insert a large needle into the horse's jugular vein, the large blood vessel that runs along each side of the neck in mammals. The needle is connected to a long tube, and soon blood begins to flow. The tube runs from the pen into a sterile room in a nearby building where the blood flows into 1.3-gallon (5 L) plastic bags. No bacteria or other harmful agents can get inside the room to contaminate the blood.

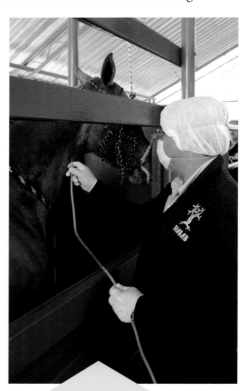

A worker at Ojo de Agua Ranch injects a horse to collect its blood. Antibodies in this blood will go on to become antivenom.

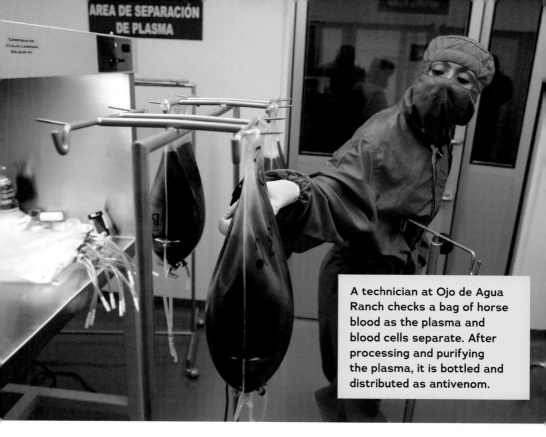

A technician at Ojo de Agua Ranch checks a bag of horse blood as the plasma and blood cells separate. After processing and purifying the plasma, it is bottled and distributed as antivenom.

After a few minutes, the bag is full. Technicians hang the bag of blood from a pole, and gravity goes to work. After a few hours, the horse blood has naturally separated, with the solid, heavy blood cells sinking to the bottom of the bag. The watery plasma remains on top. Workers pump the solid blood cells back into the horse. They save the plasma and store it in a refrigerator to move to the next step in creating antivenom.

PURIFICATION

The workers send the separated horse plasma to a pharmaceutical lab in Mexico City. Then the plasma goes through a few more steps to ensure the antibodies are refined and safe for use.

The venom antibody molecule is shaped like a Y. The two arms, known as Fab fragments, are the parts of the antibody that bind to the

THE FATHER OF ANTIVENOM

In October 1891, a young French physician named Albert Calmette (*pictured*) arrived in Saigon, the capital city of the French colony Cochinchina (modern-day Vietnam). The twenty-eight-year-old Calmette was there to help open a new branch of the Pasteur Institute, a world-renowned facility dedicated to the study of diseases. The institute was named after its founder, French chemist Louis Pasteur, a pioneer in vaccines.

Calmette's initial mission in Cochinchina was to fight diseases such as rabies and smallpox that were ravaging this part of the world. However, Calmette was also interested in other health issues specific to the region. He was particularly intrigued with the study of harmful toxins such as those in snake venom.

Cochinchina had no shortage of venomous serpents. Aggressive elapid snakes, including cobras and kraits, often terrorized the region. Shortly after Calmette arrived in Cochinchina, monsoon floods caused deadly cobras to flush from their normal habitats and invade a small village. The sudden influx of snakes among humans led to forty snakebites. In just a few days, several people died.

When Calmette arrived in Asia, no cure for venomous snakebites existed. Once envenomated, a victim could turn only to traditional medicines to ease the pain of what could eventually become a slow and painful death. The young Calmette wanted to solve this problem.

By 1894 Calmette developed the first promising snake antivenom. Calmette borrowed methods developed by a former mentor, a physician at Pasteur Institute named Emile Roux. Using hyperimmunization, Roux developed the world's first medicine to fight diphtheria, a terrible disease that affects the nose and throat.

Two years later, Calmette's antivenomous serum was saving lives in Southeast Asia and beyond. Since the days of Calmette's efforts, the field of toxicology—the study of poisonous chemicals and their effects—has come a long way. The work of many toxicologists has resulted in reliable antivenoms that fight the effects of snakes as well as scorpions, spiders, and other toxic animals. Because of his groundbreaking work, Calmette is called the Father of Antivenom.

toxin molecules, neutralizing the venom. The stem of the Y is made of horse proteins. This protein-rich stem can trigger dangerous allergic reactions if the body of a snakebite patient who receives the antivenom rejects the proteins.

For several decades, manufacturers used whole antibody molecules to make antivenoms. Up to 40 percent of antivenom patients experienced allergic reactions to the medicine. But during the 1980s, antivenom production made a giant leap forward. Scientists added an enzyme called pepsin to the antibodies. Pepsin is found in stomach acid and is good at digesting things—especially other protein molecules. Scientists discovered that pepsin could eat away the stem of the antibody protein, leaving behind the Fab fragments, the parts of the antibodies most important in fighting the effects of venom toxins. This discovery revolutionized antivenom production, and the number of patients experiencing allergic reactions plummeted during the 1990s.

After lab workers remove the protein-rich stems with the pepsin treatment, they clean and filter the antibodies several times to remove any foreign substances that may weaken the medicine. From there, they freeze-dry and bottle what is now considered antivenom. Then it is ready to ship to hospitals and medical facilities around the world.

Producing antivenom is one thing. Getting the precious drug to the communities that need it— and at a realistic cost—is another process altogether.

Once the antibodies are filtered and purified, the product is considered antivenom. The antivenom may be freeze-dried or concentrated into a powder or liquid form. It is then bottled and shipped around the world to be used to help snakebite patients.

CHAPTER 5
INTO THE SNAKE PIT

In the summer of 2015, a rattlesnake bit a middle-aged man near his home outside of San Diego, California. He sought care at a local hospital and was quickly treated with multiple vials of antivenom. The treatment was successful, and after a day or so of recovery, the man returned home. Weeks later, he received the bill for his treatment. The bill came in at $153,161.25.

What started as a crazy local story soon became national news. The Washington Post's blog ran a headline that screamed, "This $153,000 Rattlesnake Bite Is Everything Wrong with American Health Care." This claim wasn't far from the truth. The expensive treatment in San Diego wasn't an isolated event either. In 2012 a woman near Phoenix, Arizona, received a bill for more than $83,000 following antivenom treatment. In North Carolina, another bite resulted in a bill for more than $81,000. In May 2015, a Missouri man

Western diamondback rattlesnakes (*Crotalus atrox*) are found throughout the southwestern United States and northern Mexico. They are responsible for more snakebite deaths in the United States than any other snake.

died from a venomous snakebite after refusing medical treatment, claiming that he could not afford to pay for the antivenom.

In North America, the sky-high price of antivenom treatment is unique to the United States. Scorpion antivenom that costs between $7,900 and $40,000 per vial in Arizona might cost only $100 across the border in Mexico. So why is antivenom so expensive in the United States?

Not long after these stories of outrageous bills for antivenom treatment made national headlines, Leslie Boyer sat down to figure out why one vial of antivenom costs so much in the United States. Boyer cobbled together data on expenses from various sources involved in each step of antivenom production—from the costs of research in the United States to the production ranch in Mexico, to local hospital pharmacists and health insurance providers. Boyer then used the data to create a model that would break down the cost of producing a vial of antivenom, piece by piece and dollar by dollar. In her model, the final price of one vial of antivenom in the United States was $14,624.

Boyer found that research and production of the medicine make up only a fraction of the final price. The cost of producing snake antivenom—including collecting snake venom, extracting plasma, and bottling the medicine—accounts for only about 0.1 percent, or $140, of the final antivenom price tag.

About $4,100 of the vial's price—about 28 percent—comes from the lengthy and expensive process of manufacturing and distributing antivenom. This includes research and development, clinical trials, legal fees, marketing, taxes, and other costs associated with making a safe and effective drug. Finally, the vast majority of that final bill—about $9,800, or 70 percent—comes from the unique (and very complex) structure of the American health-care system.

CLINICAL TRIALS

Once a drug manufacturer develops a new drug, the company must seek approval by the US Food and Drug Administration (FDA) before it can hit the market. One of the most important steps in drug approval is clinical trials, where new medicines are tested to make sure they are safe and effective.

The first trials are preclinical—the new drugs are tested on animals in a laboratory. If the new drug is found to be safe and effective in this stage, it moves on to be tested on humans in a series of clinical trials. Phase 1 of human trials requires a small sample of volunteers. Those running the trial identify and monitor the drug's side effects. For example, they must find out if the drug causes people to become sick or break out in a rash.

Phase 2 of the trial requires hundreds of volunteers. In this phase, those running the trial test the drug's effectiveness on different types of patients. The trial may test how the drug affects people who smoke or people who have another unrelated illness. Finally, in phase 3, thousands of participants test different doses of the drug or test how it works with other drugs. Manufacturers continue to monitor a drug's safety once the medicine hits the market and is used by patients.

HEALTH CARE IN THE UNITED STATES

Check out any news source and you'll likely see a story about the American health-care system. Headlines will say it's too big, it's too expensive, it's broken, or it just doesn't work. All of these statements have some truth in them, and the price of antivenom in the United States is a useful snapshot of the health-care system as a whole. Health care is big business in the United States. As of 2015, the last year for which data was available, spending on health care in the United States accounted for about 17.8 percent of the US economy. That's about twice as much as the United Kingdom spends on its health care.

In its simplest form, the US health-care market works like this: If a person gets sick or has a small injury, that person will seek treatment from a doctor or nurse. That treatment costs money. The patient seeking help must pay for the goods and services received, such as medicine, stitches, or X-rays. The patient also pays for the doctor and nurse who provides care, an examination, and advice. If the injury or sickness is more significant—say a broken arm or a life-threatening disease such as cancer—the price of these goods and services can get very expensive very quickly.

These prices can also vary widely from hospital to hospital and from state to state. In 2013 the *Huffington Post* news site used data from the Centers for Medicare and Medicaid Services database to examine the price of treatment in the New York City area for a common heart condition. One hospital in suburban New Jersey billed treatment at $99,690 per patient. Meanwhile, at a hospital in the Bronx, one of New York's five boroughs, just 20 miles (32 km) away, the same treatment was just $7,044 per patient.

In the United States, nearly 90 percent of people have health insurance in some form, according to data released by the Centers for Disease Control and Prevention (CDC) in 2017. Americans get health insurance in a number of ways. More than half of Americans get health insurance through their employer. About one-third of Americans get their insurance through Medicaid or Medicare, two massive government programs that provide aid to low-income people or people of retirement age (sixty-five years and older) and some with disabilities or certain illnesses. About 10 percent of Americans purchase a health insurance plan directly from an insurance provider. These people are usually self-employed or for some reason do not have insurance through an employer or the government. Purchasing directly from an insurance company is usually very expensive. Not everybody in the United States has health insurance, however. About 10 percent of Americans go without, either because they choose not to buy it or because they simply cannot afford the price of coverage.

WHO PAYS FOR WHAT?

Regardless of how a person gets health insurance, most people pay a monthly or yearly sum—a premium—to the insurance provider, either directly or through the employer or the government. Insurance providers are then able to build a large pool of money from the millions of people and companies contributing to their insurance plans. If a person in the insurance pool becomes sick, the pool of money built up from all the premiums will pay for some portion of the medical treatment and prescription drugs that person receives. Doctors and hospitals then bill the insurance providers, which draw from that pool of money to pay for the cost of goods (medicine and supplies) and services (office visits, surgeries, and lab work) a person might need during a health emergency.

Most health insurance policies have a schedule of benefits. This schedule lists the medical procedures covered under the health-care plan. Health insurance usually has limits to how much an insurer will pay for various procedures. And policies may have lifetime limits to how much the insurer will pay for a single person. Once the patient reaches any of those limits, the remaining costs fall to the patient.

Insurance providers also have networks, or contracts with doctors and hospitals to provide service. If a patient gets medical help from within that network, the cost of service is at one level. The insurance provider may pay all of that cost or a significant portion of it. If the patient chooses service outside that network, the cost of service can increase significantly. This sometimes happens when a patient needs a particular type of service that is not available in the network. In the out-of-network scenario, the provider may not pay for any of the cost or it may pay for a much smaller percentage of the cost.

Between premiums, schedules of benefits, networks, and other variables, the goods and services covered under a health insurance policy—and how much it will cost—varies greatly. Depending on a person's plan, a snakebite and antivenom treatment might not be covered. A patient may not know this unless the patient asks up front—or if a snakebite occurs and the bill shows up in the mail weeks after treatment.

AN UNLEVELED PLAYING FIELD

Health insurance providers are in constant negotiations with drug manufacturers and medical providers. Drug manufacturers and health-care providers tell insurance companies how much they will charge for their goods and services. In return, the insurance company tells them how much they will actually pay for those goods and services. These negotiations go back and forth, usually starting at a very high price and then slowly trickling down to a price both parties agree on. These negotiations decide the final price for products and services provided during treatment.

Not all patient pools are equal—at least in the eyes of the American health-care industry. Health insurance programs such as Medicare and Medicaid generally pay doctors and hospitals much less than larger for-profit insurance companies such as United Healthcare or Humana do. This unequal system has real-life consequences. Take, for example, some parts of the Bronx, New York. One neighborhood in the Bronx might have a higher percentage of elderly or low-income residents relying on Medicaid or Medicare for health care. Because these programs pay health providers less, the neighborhood might not attract big hospitals or the best doctors. Meanwhile, just a few miles away in a wealthy suburb of New Jersey, more people will have health insurance programs that pay their medical providers a better rate. This, in turn, attracts the best facilities and doctors. The areas that need the best medical providers often lose out to wealthier areas.

THE PRICE OF SAFE MEDICINE

Manufacturing and distributing a lifesaving medicine is complex. It takes years of research and development and millions of dollars of investment. Tests, clinical trials, laws, and regulations all ensure the drugs are safe and effective. However, the US government did not always regulate drug research, development, and manufacture, and it came with a price.

In 1901 thirteen children died in Saint Louis, Missouri, after they were given a diphtheria antitoxin tainted with tetanus, a potentially deadly bacterium. Several months later, another nine children died after receiving an unclean smallpox vaccine. The reaction to these tragedies was swift, and the US Congress passed the Biologics Control Act of 1902. This law set safety standards for commercially produced medicines such as vaccines and antitoxins. For the first time in US history, pharmaceuticals were regulated.

Over time, many laws followed to improve drug manufacturing in the United States. In 1906, for example, a new law established a powerful government agency to protect consumers through the regulation of food and drugs in the United States. The agency would eventually become the Food and Drug Administration.

The FDA has rigorous health and safety standards for the production of medicines. Drug manufacturers must follow these standards and prove a medicine's safety and effectiveness to get approval from the FDA for the sale and distribution of any new drug. Following the standards is expensive, and they apply to every step of production.

The costs of meeting such high standards can add up quickly. In the case of antivenom production, they start with research and development in VIPER and other laboratories, where researchers work to identify new and potent forms of the antivenom drug. The care and housing of venom-donating snakes and blood-donating mammals such as the horses at Alagón's ranch cost money. So does safely bottling and packaging antivenom. And then there's the costs of clinical trials, first on animals and then on human test subjects. On top of it all, huge costs from packaging, reviews, inspections, marketing, taxes, and other fees all contribute to the final price tag of safe and effective antivenom.

On average, the FDA will approve fewer than 10 percent of all new drugs. The other 90 percent are failures. And failure means a lot of time and money went into developing a medicine that never makes it to market, never sells, and never earns a profit. When it takes hundreds of millions of dollars to develop medicines, that's a huge loss for a drug manufacturer. So companies roll their losses into the cost of developing drugs that do make it to market. And they sometimes increase the price of a successful drug to cover the risk of investing in future products that may fail.

In the United States, the pharmaceutical industry is very powerful. Experts predict that by 2020 American citizens will spend an estimated $610 billion on prescription drugs. Each year the companies that make these drugs bring in billions of dollars in profits. A percentage of these profits goes toward efforts to ensure that Americans will continue buying the product. For example, pharmaceutical companies may donate funds to doctors, researchers, and politicians to encourage them to support specific pharmaceutical products and goals. The companies also hire lobbyists to work with politicians on legislation that supports pharmaceutical interests. In general, when it comes to producing and marketing drugs, pharmaceutical companies focus on the products and channels that will bring in the largest profits.

Hospitals also make sure they can recover losses from money spent on specialized drugs such as antivenom. In the United States, hospitals must treat snakebite patients whether or not the patient can pay for the treatment. If a victim can't pay the bill or doesn't have health insurance to help cover the expenses, a hospital can lose tens of thousands of dollars from treating a snakebite patient. So hospitals crank up the prices on rare drugs to help pay for those losses.

SUPPLY AND DEMAND

Another major factor in the price of antivenom is supply and demand. This set of economic laws determines the prices for most goods and services in a capitalist economy where individuals own and operate most companies. The number of people who want or need a product (demand) and the amount of that product that is available to them (supply) determine the price of that product. For example, if petroleum refineries reduce the amount of gasoline they produce (the supply), yet the number of people who need gas does not go down (the demand), the price of gas will climb. But if those petroleum refineries ramp up production of gasoline and flood the market with supply, the price of that product will drop as manufacturers compete for gasoline sales.

The basic laws of supply and demand are also at play with antivenom. Most Americans do not live near venomous snakes. So venomous snakebites are rare, and the demand for antivenom is low. Without a high demand for antivenom in the United States, the price of that product will remain very high. For most drug manufacturers, the meager profits gained from providing antivenom just aren't worth the cost of producing the product.

THE GREAT SNAKE OIL SALESMAN

The term *snake oil salesman* describes someone who is a scammer, or a huckster. This person sells a fraudulent product hoping to make a quick buck off gullible customers. The origins of this term are in the history of antivenom.

During the 1890s, hucksters selling miracle medicines could easily exploit the public. Few if any consumer protection laws existed to shield people from fraudulent products and claims. By the turn of the century, a whole host of curious drugs hit the market, each claiming fantastic cures. One such drug was Clark Stanley's Snake Oil Liniment.

Clark Stanley (born in 1854) was a native of Texas. He billed himself as the Rattlesnake King and boasted a magical cure-all that he said he alone could produce. All he needed was a rattlesnake and an audience who wanted to believe. The Rattlesnake King first gained fame during the 1893 World Expo in Chicago, Illinois, where he put on a spectacular show for curious crowds. During his act, Stanley dazzled onlookers by handling a live rattlesnake and then killing it and squeezing the snake's body to produce an oily goo. This goo, he claimed, was the secret ingredient in his snake oil—a miraculous medicine hidden away inside a deadly viper. Stanley claimed his snake oil would cure common maladies from sore throats to sprains and even paralysis.

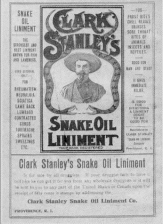

This advertisement for Clark Stanley's Snake Oil Liniment claims that the potion gives relief for toothaches, back pain, and frostbite.

For years, Stanley made a fortune off his Snake Oil Liniment. But in 1906, Congress passed the Federal Food and Drug Act. The law was the first real attempt to shut down the many fraudulent, misbranded drugs that were widespread across the nation. In 1916 the law caught up with Stanley. Federal investigators seized a shipment of his potion. They found that his Snake Oil Liniment was actually composed of mineral oil, beef fat, camphor, and turpentine. It didn't have a drop of rattlesnake oil.

Stanley admitted his wrongdoing and accepted his punishment: a fine of $20. In 2017 dollars, that's about $500—a slap on the hand. All the same, Stanley's snake oil empire had finally come to an embarrassing end, but not before swindling thousands out of their cash.

CHAPTER 6
A GLOBAL PERSPECTIVE

The market forces that create high costs of antivenom in the United States are the same forces that fan the flames of the Vicious Circle around the world. In the United States, demand for antivenom is low because there just aren't that many snakebites each year. Meanwhile, in other parts of the world, demand for antivenom is very high. Venomous snakes bite hundreds of thousands of people in Africa and Asia each year. However, the supply of antivenom is low in these countries for a number of social, economic, and cultural reasons.

The international antivenom market can be wildly unpredictable. Drug manufacturers need dependable markets to justify the massive investment into research, development, and production of medicines. Yet the regions most in need of antivenom are usually in low-income nations. Antivenom producers cannot be certain the people and hospitals in these parts of the world will be able to pay for the product. The drug manufacturers also can't be sure that these hospitals will buy antivenom in large enough quantities to make it profitable to produce the medicine. So the supply of antivenom is often choked off.

When fighting an international health crisis, the roller-coaster supply of key medicines can have devastating and long-lasting effects. In sub-Saharan Africa, the snakebite health crisis first went into overdrive during the late 1990s when several large antivenom producers ended production. Most cited the lack of a predictable market and problems with payment by government agencies. They also said they faced stiff competition from illegal markets that were selling antivenoms inexpensively. Even though these black market medicines were less than effective, they were affordable.

The decline in production left a large gap between supply and demand. The supply of antivenom plummeted while the demand remained constant. By 1998 fewer than one hundred thousand vials of antivenom were available throughout Africa. These vials would have met less than 25 percent of the overall demand across the African continent.

WHO STEPS IN

As the crisis worsened in the early twenty-first century, the world—in particular the World Health Organization—began to notice. Part of the United Nations, WHO is an international alliance of government health agencies that combat global health issues. They focus on diseases such as HIV/AIDS, Ebola, malaria, heart disease, and cancer around the world. Active in more than 150 countries, WHO often brings much-needed attention, money, and resources to overlooked health issues such as venomous snakebites. WHO can also hire medical workers and researchers from all over the world to help areas that are fighting large-scale health problems.

In 2009, after much lobbying by medical professionals, WHO finally listed venomous snakebite as a neglected tropical disease

(NTD). On this list are diseases such as dengue fever, leprosy, and rabies. Compared to widespread epidemics such as HIV/AIDS or malaria, these diseases don't affect as many people. But they can still be devastating to the communities where they occur. Most NTDs plague poor regions with few medical resources. And this is exactly where venomous snakes are most common.

Bringing attention to rare or neglected diseases is often an early and critical step in solving a problem. And the increased awareness of the snakebite crisis did eventually help increase the supply of antivenom. Several private producers jumped back into the game, and by 2012, about twelve antivenom products were available in Africa. However, the supply of the medicine was still below what was necessary to cover the estimated three hundred thousand to five hundred thousand snakebite victims in Africa each year.

FAV-AFRIQUE

Eventually, instability crept back into the African antivenom market. For several years, the French private pharmaceutical company Sanofi Pasteur had produced a highly effective and popular antivenom known as Fav-Afrique. This potent antivenom used venom antibodies from ten different venomous snake species common to sub-Saharan Africa. Fav-Afrique was widely regarded as one of the most reliable and effective antivenoms in sub-Saharan Africa. During the development of the drug, Fav-Afrique went through rigorous testing and clinical trials by the Stringent Regulatory Authority, the French equivalent to the FDA. These measures helped ensure that Fav-Afrique was safe and effective. But the drug was extremely expensive because of the thorough and slow process. Ultimately, some countries were unable to afford the drug.

Since the early twenty-first century, when Fav-Afrique was first available in Africa, some nations tried to cut corners to save money. In 2003 the West African nation of Ghana was experiencing a rash

By some estimates, the West African carpet viper is responsible for more than ten thousand deadly bites each year in West Africa. Antivenom has proven effective in treating carpet viper bites, but there is a shortage of antivenom in West African nations.

of deadly venomous snakebites from the West African carpet viper (*Echis ocellatus*). The venom from this common viper has hemotoxins that stop blood from clotting. Ghana's Ministry of Health was the government agency responsible for purchasing antivenoms. Following the spike in the number of snakebites, the ministry replaced its supply of Fav-Afrique with another less expensive antivenom produced in India. The results were devastating. Over a three-year period, death rates from the new, less effective antivenom were six times higher than that of Fav-Afrique.

With fewer sales and slim profits, Sanofi Pasteur halted production of its antivenom in 2014, and the last batches of Fav-Afrique expired in 2016. This contributed to yet another dip in antivenom supplies in Africa.

ANOTHER VICIOUS CIRCLE

Snakebite shares many traits with other crises such as HIV/AIDS, malaria, or tuberculosis that affect marginalized communities around the world. These health epidemics are not limited to faraway places. Many of the problems that fuel the snakebite crisis also drive the drug addiction epidemic ravaging parts of the United States. Opioids are powerful painkilling drugs that can be highly addictive. Opioids can be legal drugs prescribed by a doctor, such as the drug fentanyl, or they can be illegal substances such as heroin. The widespread use of both legal and illegal opioids has seen a massive increase in recent years, and the problem shows no sign of slowing down. In 2016 opioid drugs were responsible for more than forty-two thousand drug overdose deaths in the United States alone.

The people and places most affected by opioids are often rural, poor, and underserved communities. These areas lack resources such as inexpensive and reliable medical care. Education and outreach programs—counselors and drug addiction facilities—are often lacking as well. Looming over all of this is a massive health-care system that emphasizes profits over people. The opioid epidemic in the United States faces its own Vicious Circle that requires many resources such as money, education, and assistance from government agencies, private businesses, and international aid organizations to defeat.

A SCORPION'S STING

Mexico is home to a spellbinding array of native venomous species. They include snakes, scorpions, spiders, and Gila monsters. Some parts of Mexico are remote. They are often poor and lack resources and effective medical facilities such as clinics and hospitals. By the 1980s, Mexico had all the ingredients for its own Vicious Circle as the annual rate of scorpion stings seemed as if it was going to spiral out of control.

About 280 species of scorpions are native to Mexico. This is more than 10 percent of all known scorpion species worldwide. Each year around the country, tens of thousands of scorpion sting victims seek treatment in health facilities. The real number may be even higher.

Many scorpion stings go unreported each year too because not all communities have health-care facilities. By the 1990s, Mexico was reporting about three hundred scorpion-related deaths each year. Most of those deaths were infants or small children.

In the early 1990s, several Mexican manufacturers of scorpion antivenom were making low-quality, ineffective medicines. People in rural areas who needed help when stung often did not trust the local medical workers or their medicines. Sound familiar? Mexico was living through its own Vicious Circle.

THE SCORPION PROBLEM

Scorpions are eight-legged arachnids, the class of invertebrate animals that includes spiders, ticks, and mites. Scorpions are some of the oldest creatures on Earth, dating back some 430 million years. These days about fifteen hundred species of scorpions are found around the world, mostly in arid and dry environments such as America's desert Southwest or the vast Sahara in Africa.

All scorpions are predators and possess venomous stings. For a healthy adult, a scorpion's sting is mostly just a very painful and unpleasant experience, but for young children, elderly adults, or those who suffer from other health issues, a scorpion sting can be life-threatening. Each year, an estimated 1.2 million scorpion stings occur, resulting in about three thousand deaths, often in regions that lack medical resources to treat the stings. In parts of South America, the Middle East, and India, scorpion stings are a major health concern.

Scorpions from the family Hadrurus are the largest scorpions in North America. They live in the United States and Mexico. Their stings are painful but are typically not dangerous.

This changed in 1995 when the toddler son of Mexico's president, Ernesto Zedillo, was stung by a scorpion. The boy was rushed to the hospital in a desperate fight to save his life. Zedillo and his family lived in Mexico City, a sprawling metropolis where scorpions are not common. The doctors at the hospital were at a loss. They were untrained and uneducated on how to treat scorpion stings. And the hospital did not have a supply of reliable scorpion antivenom.

Luckily, one doctor at the hospital happened to have a vial of one of the more effective scorpion antivenoms on the market. With time and options running out, he gave the boy the scorpion antivenom. In just a matter of minutes, the boy was recovering.

Following this near tragedy, Zedillo wanted to know more about the scorpion sting situation in Mexico. The doctors explained that scorpion stings are common in rural parts of Mexico and that ineffective antivenoms and untrained medical workers were creating a nationwide scorpion sting epidemic. The scorpion menace was an everyday threat for Mexicans in rural areas, and many children were

Ernesto Zedillo was president of Mexico from 1994 to 2000. During his presidency, he addressed the scorpion epidemic through education programs and government funding for antivenom production. His commitment to the problem was fueled by his son's experience with a near-fatal scorpion bite.

With the president's experience, the wealthy and powerful in Mexico took notice of the scorpion problem. The government formed workshops to train medical workers throughout the nation to treat stings. Education programs received money to teach more Mexicans how and where to find treatment for scorpion stings. Outreach programs worked to build trust between communities and medical workers. Government agencies gave money to manufacturers to subsidize—help pay for—antivenom production. The quality of the drugs increased too. Supplies of these antivenoms were distributed more effectively to doctors and hospitals in rural areas.

The results were immediate, and over the next decade, the scorpion epidemic ended. Annual deaths from scorpion stings plummeted from about three hundred per year in 1992 to twenty-five per year by 2007. The numbers have not increased since then.

Thanks to a cooperative effort, Mexico stopped its own Vicious Circle. It wasn't easy, it wasn't perfect, and it wasn't cheap. But it saved lives, and it helped reverse a national health crisis that was rapidly spiraling out of control. Government and private companies worked together—in investment, research, outreach, and education—so that Mexico could attack every part of its scorpion epidemic at the same time. These lessons may help turn the tide of snakebite's Vicious Circle.

CHAPTER 7
REVERSING THE VICIOUS CIRCLE

The Vicious Circle does not have one simple cause, nor does it have one simple solution. To reverse it, "You have to hit everything at once," says Boyer. Combating the Vicious Circle takes a coordinated effort, at international and local levels. For starters, WHO took the important first step of raising awareness of the problem. In 2009 WHO declared snakebite to be a neglected tropical disease. The next year, the organization released Guidelines for the Prevention and Clinical Management of Snakebite in Africa. This manual for doctors and other medical workers helped standardize snakebite diagnosis, treatment, and care for bites from a variety of snake species. The manual provides guidelines for how to properly apply and store antivenoms. It also stresses the need to increase reporting and record keeping. WHO's guidelines were a giant leap forward.

Shortly after the guidelines came out, an Australia-based nonprofit organization launched the Global Snakebite Initiative (GSI). Led by snakebite experts from around the world, the initiative manages a large network of medical workers, policy makers, and other individuals and organizations to stop the Vicious Circle. The initiative works in nations such as Kenya and Swaziland that are hit hard by the snakebite crisis. Its workers there help to make sure that communities have effective antivenoms. They also train people to treat snakebite victims so that fewer people die, and they help patients through rehabilitation.

Meanwhile, many nations around the world have signed an agreement called the Pharmaceutical Inspection Co-operation Scheme (PIC/S), an international agreement between the national drug

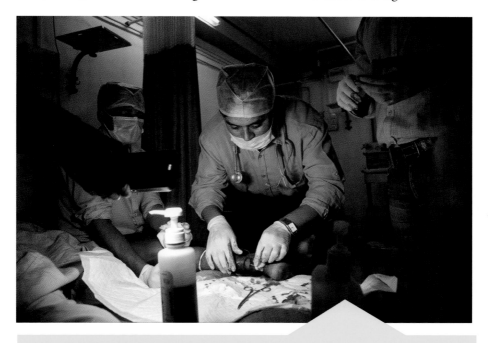

Dr. Ganesh Rakh treats a snakebite patient in a hospital in Pune, India. In 2010 WHO published guidelines for snakebite treatment that are specific to the needs of doctors and patients in India and the surrounding region.

administration agencies of the member nations. More than fifty other nations participate in the PIC/S agreement, including the United States, Australia, the United Kingdom, France, and much of South America. Each of these member nations is responsible for following PIC/S guidelines to regulate the manufacture and distribution of medicine in their own country. They must meet high standards for producing antivenom medicine that is safe and effective for human use. For example, labs and manufacturing facilities of PIC/S participants go through rigorous inspections for health and safety. This regulation ensures that medicines are safe and effective before they reach customers—no matter what part of the world they are shipped to.

Antivenom and other medicines are often slow to reach communities in need because safety regulations vary so much from country to country. Medicines produced cheaply and quickly in Mexico might not meet the safety standards of the FDA in the United States. So the drugs will have to go through more tests before the FDA will approve them for sale. And medicines produced in the United States might have to meet different standards in places such as Sweden or France. This will require additional testing before the American drugs can be sold in Europe. Meeting these various standards takes time and money, ultimately slowing the supply chain of critical medicines.

PIC/S is an attempt to establish one set of international standards. Manufacturers in member nations must meet only one set of very high standards. Once they have met these standards, the producers can sell their medicine around the world to other PIC/S nations—without additional testing, so antivenom and other medicines can get to communities in need quickly.

In 2018 Mexico's Federal Commission for the Protection of Sanitary Risk (COFEPRIS) became a PIC/S member. (The commission is the Mexican equivalent to the FDA.) So Mexico's antivenom manufacturers now have greater access to international markets. In turn, other nations have access to Mexico's inexpensive antivenom. Many leaders hope that Mexico's success in defeating its scorpion sting crisis will translate to the world stage to help crush the Vicious Circle in the world of snakebites.

PRIMING THE PUMP

Awareness, education, and standard treatments and regulations are just part of the solution to the Vicious Circle. The next step in combating the snakebite crisis is to make sure that nations have access to the supplies of antivenom that they need—and at a reasonable cost. Many experts believe that governments must work with private companies to make this happen. Boyer suggests that kick-starting investment in antivenom supplies might be a smart first step. "Where there are shortages, you need to prime the pump," she says. "You need investment from Ministries of Health where, for a few years, drugs are going to be subsidized [paid for by the government and private organizations] and . . . in large enough quantity that hospitals are going to have a reliable source."

Subsidizing a medicine and having trained workers in place to give treatment can go a long way toward reversing the Vicious Circle. For example, government health-care agencies and international organizations can purchase large quantities of antivenom from private manufacturers. Drug manufacturers are therefore willing to invest in making the medicine because they know they have consumers (the agencies and the organizations) that want the drugs and that have the money to pay for them.

With effective medicines and trained medical workers who know how to use them, communities with snakebite outbreaks are more likely to trust the treatment. They begin to seek help more regularly when a snakebite occurs. With this better relationship, patients will come into hospitals and pay for proper treatment, knowing that the drugs work. As a result, hospitals and other medical facilities will eventually purchase more antivenom and keep more in stock, knowing that the community will come to them for treatment of snakebites.

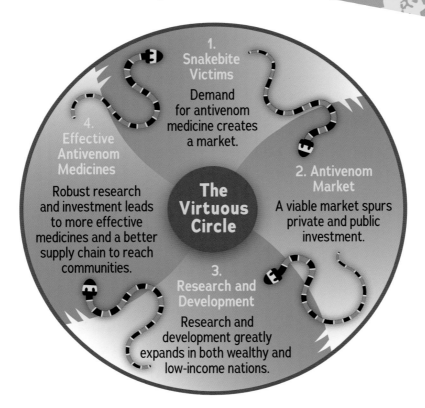

The Virtuous Circle

1. **Snakebite Victims**
Demand for antivenom medicine creates a market.

2. **Antivenom Market**
A viable market spurs private and public investment.

3. **Research and Development**
Research and development greatly expands in both wealthy and low-income nations.

4. **Effective Antivenom Medicines**
Robust research and investment leads to more effective medicines and a better supply chain to reach communities.

Only when each part of the Vicious Circle is attacked at once can the deadly cycle of snakebite be reversed. In the Virtuous Circle, trust is built between communities and medical workers. Then drug manufacturers commit to producing reliable and affordable medicines. This balance of supply and demand ensures that effective medicines will get to the people who need them most.

Within a few years, the market is self-sustaining and government investment can be reduced. With this established relationship, private drug manufacturers now have a reliable market, helping to ensure that production of effective medicines will continue. It's a cycle that feeds itself.

EMPOWERING PEOPLE

Another important part of reversing the Vicious Circle is to improve education about snakes and snakebites. On-the-ground training and education in areas where snakebites are widespread are key. These efforts help communities with few resources build trust with medicines and medical workers. Training includes teaching those workers how to identify snakebites, how to choose the right medicines, and how to give the right dose of antivenom. It also includes teaching people how to care for snakebite patients after treatment.

Boyer herself takes this matter to heart. Over the course of several years, she has developed a series of instructional videos that are being used in rural hospitals and other medical facilities in sub-Saharan Africa and elsewhere. These videos help train medical professionals about proper and effective snakebite treatment.

Media such as radio, television, and the internet play a critical role in training and education too. Radio broadcasting has been a very effective tool in reaching rural African communities. Pamphlets and posters are also effective for bringing the message directly to the people.

The VIPER Institute, led by Leslie Boyer, partnered with experts from Mexico and Africa to develop a series of videos to educate African health-care professionals about venom, antivenom, and treatment of snakebite patients. Boyer and her partners are also working with government and industry leaders to make high-quality, affordable antivenom available in sub-Saharan Africa.

SNAKE SAFETY

Snakes are amazing and fascinating creatures, but they mostly want to be left alone. Be cautious when walking in an area where snakes live. Wear shoes and carry a flashlight when traveling at night. Try to avoid snakes so you don't cause them to strike in self-defense. If a snakebite does occur, here are a few steps to take immediately following the bite:

- Don't panic. Never jump or run away quickly. This will increase your heart rate, increasing the flow of blood around the body, and causing the venom to spread more quickly. Remain calm. Then get to a medical facility as quickly as possible.

- Remove any jewelry or tight clothing in the area of the bite that could inhibit blood flow or cause pain if the area begins to swell.

- Clean the bite area, but don't flush it with water. Do not apply ice or a cold compress. This could cause more damage to the bite area.

- If possible, take a photograph of the snake—but only from a safe distance! If you don't have a camera, try to note any markings, colors, or patterns on the snake. Identifying the right species of snake can help medical workers make informed choices about treatment. Whatever you do, do not pursue the snake.

- Antivenom is the only effective cure for snakebites. Seek medical assistance as quickly as possible by calling 911 or going to a hospital.

While hiking in areas with snakes, be sure to wear long pants, socks, and hiking boots. Trekking poles are useful in pushing vegetation out of the way so you can avoid stepping on a snake accidentally.

Although the internet is a valuable teaching tool, reliable access to the internet is not always available or reliable in many of the regions most affected by snakebites.

The ultimate goal is to improve the outcome for people with snakebites in Africa, not only to reduce the number of annual bites but also to ensure more people survive these accidents. "In order to do that, we need multiple things to happen," Boyer explains. "But the one we're working on is the education of doctors and nurses. We want the people who take care of snake-bitten patients to know the latest and best information on what snake venom is, how it affects the body, [and] how we can stop it from causing harm."

"FOLLOWING THE MOLECULE"

The people who fight the Vicious Circle are often involved in more than one way and have many areas of knowledge. Boyer says, "Many people have to cross over and serve as experts in more than one area." She points out that in combating an international NTD, "it's really essential for us to understand the language the other ones speak, both the language of science and medicine, and the language of people— French, Spanish, English, and African languages."

Boyer refers to this type of involvement as "following the molecule." She is a medical doctor, researcher, and educator. She might train doctors in Africa on the proper treatment of snakebites. She might meet with government officials in Washington, DC, to help shape policy. She might also meet with other scientists from around the world at a WHO conference in Geneva, Switzerland. Boyer might be at the herpetarium in Mexico with graduate students collecting venom from rare snakes. "Then I get to meet the cowboy who takes care of the horses at the ranch," she explains. "And then I get to meet the little boy in Africa whose life is saved by that very horse's serum. *That* is cool."

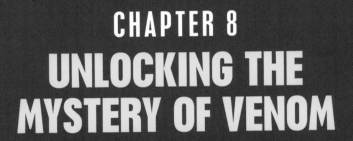

CHAPTER 8
UNLOCKING THE MYSTERY OF VENOM

How will the snakebite crisis story end? Will the Vicious Circle be defeated? Experts say a lot of work is left to do. Ending the Vicious Circle might take years or even decades. And it could flare up again. The solutions that work one day might not fix the problems we face the next day.

Global climate change, for example, may one day impact the snakebite crisis. As the climate grows warmer and drier, food sources and habitats will change. Some of the animals will adapt to these changing environments. Others will die off or move into other areas to survive. Snakes are no exception. As climate change impacts their natural habitats, they will have to adapt to survive. This might mean moving into new areas that have never seen venomous snakes before.

Timber rattlesnakes have been extinct in Ontario, Canada, since 1941. But some experts predict that with climate change, the snakes could move back into Ontario and other Canadian provinces by 2050 as the climate warms in these regions.

For example, the timber rattlesnake (*Crotalus horridus*) is the most widespread venomous snake in the eastern United States. It lives as far north as New England and as far south as Florida. With climate change already impacting the United States, this snake species may soon move farther north into central Canada as the climate there becomes friendlier to cold-blooded reptiles.

Humans are on the move too. The worldwide human population in 1900 was less than 2 billion people. By December 2017, it had reached an estimated 7.6 billion. By the year 2050 the human population may approach 10 billion. And all of those people need food, water, and safe places to live. That's a lot of additional stress on an environment that is already nearing a breaking point.

As the planet's population grows, humans are clearing away large areas of forests and grasslands to use for growing crops, raising livestock, and building new communities. Removing forests and other habitats increases the likelihood of contact between people and wild animals, such as snakes. And as humans move into previously untouched snake habitats, the risk of snakebites will greatly increase. Even a small spike in the number of venomous bites each year could result in tens of thousands more deaths worldwide.

Furthermore, human conflicts around the globe create an unstable world that has dire consequences for ending the Vicious Circle. War, terrorism, and political instability can choke off the supply of medical drugs and medical care reaching the communities in need. In some conflicts, such as the ongoing civil war in Syria, armies actually target hospitals and clinics to kill civilians. Doctors Without Borders is one of many nonprofit organizations that provides medical care to poor or war-torn communities around the world. During times of unrest, they are often in harm's way. They may be forced to evacuate a region and will no longer be able to work with these communities. Combating venomous snakebite in these circumstances is almost impossible.

VENOMICS

The snakebite crisis is serious and will be difficult to overcome. However, researchers do see bright spots in the future. Venom is an extraordinarily complex mixture of chemicals that scientists have only begun to understand. Mysterious venom molecules might still be inside this toxic brew waiting to be discovered. Thanks to major advances in the field of genetics (the study of how genes define physical and behavioral characteristics), scientists have started to study venom molecules to understand how and why they work. The mystery of venom has opened up an entirely new field of science called venomics, which explores venom's potential for use in other medications. Venomics helps categorize the vast library of venom molecules hidden away in the thousands of venomous creatures found around Earth.

Venom holds the potential to save lives precisely because it is so effective as a killer. Venom works instantly and attacks its targets with incredible precision. These are the very same characteristics of an effective medicine. Scientists working in the lab break down venom into its individual parts, and they isolate the hundreds of different types of molecules that make up the toxic soup. As they begin to understand how each molecule works and what it does, researchers are already turning deadly venom into lifesaving medicines.

Even since the early 1950s, snake venom has been used to help combat some diseases. For example, the Brazilian viper (*Bothrops jararaca*) has a deadly venom with strong blood-thinning qualities that cause its victims to bleed to death. When deconstructed, or pulled apart, in the lab, scientists discovered that some of the molecules in this viper's deadly venom contain peptides, short chains of organic compounds called amino acids. Pharmaceutical companies use the peptides to create a lifesaving medicine known as an angiotensin-converting enzyme (ACE) inhibitor. This drug causes blood vessels to relax and allows blood cells to flow more easily. These inhibitors, approved by the FDA for public use in 1981, revolutionized the treatment of high blood pressure and heart failure. In the twenty-first century, they are used around the world.

Lab workers extract venom from a pit viper at the Butantan Institute in Sao Paulo, Brazil. The institute has been working for more than one hundred years to research and produce antivenom and other medications and vaccines.

Who knows what other cures are locked away in snake venom? Researchers at the University of Southern California in Los Angeles are experimenting with the toxins in some rattlesnake venom that attack red blood cells. Harnessing the power and precision of these toxins might help destroy tumor cells in aggressive forms of cancer. Meanwhile, scientists at Universidad Central del Caribe in Puerto Rico are experimenting with the neurotoxic venoms from elapids such as mambas. The nerve-destroying elements of this venom show promise in slowing the effects of Parkinson's disease, a life-threatening condition that attacks the brain and nervous system.

The potential for venom as a lifesaver is not limited to snakes, either. Remember the deadliest of them all, the cone snail from the South Pacific Ocean? New medicines based on a peptide in this animal's venom have led to effective painkillers. The cone snail's venom molecules are unusual because they don't need to be altered or synthesized (artificially made) to create the painkilling drug. Most drugs based on animal molecules are broken down, reengineered, or synthesized before they're used in medicines. Unlike opioid-based drugs, this drug derived directly from the cone snail venom is not addictive. It helps people who suffer from chronic, untreatable pain by blocking neuron channels. The drug has to be injected into the spine, however, and is not as easy to take as painkilling pills.

The Gila monster is a venomous reptile that is widespread in Arizona and New Mexico. Beginning in 2006, researchers used chemicals in Gila monster saliva to create several different drugs that regulate the release of insulin. This hormone helps balance blood sugar levels in our bodies. The FDA approved these medicines, which are effective for people with diabetes.

How about the venom molecules in common beestings? The proteins packed into bee venom cause terrible pain in sting victims. The venom proteins attack cell membranes in the skin, causing them to explode. Researchers at Washington University in Saint Louis,

Missouri, have found that bee venom toxins attack the protective membrane surrounding HIV cells. In large enough doses, the bee venom components can destroy the HIV cells before they infect a person. This could be a big step forward in combating the virus, which causes AIDS, a disease that has killed more than thirty-five million people worldwide in recent decades.

Venoms are also showing promise in other ways. Researchers are testing scorpion venom as a key ingredient in a chemical to identify cancer cells that aren't seen during surgery to remove cancerous tumors. In the lab, some scorpion venom has been shown to stick to cancer cells while they do not stick to healthy cells. When mixed with a bright dye, these venom molecules light up cancer cells so surgeons can target them for removal.

THE SIXTH WAVE

The field of venomics is relatively new. Fully understanding venom will take years or even generations before we can truly harness the power of these toxins. This potential is precisely why it is important to protect all species of snakes and other animals—even the venomous ones.

Yet ever since humans began contemplating their role in the natural world, we have mostly thought of snakes as our enemies. Many species of snakes are dangerous, and some are deadly. But venomous snakes aren't really the problem.

In the several billion years that life has existed on Earth, five mass extinctions have claimed thousands—if not millions—of species, including all the dinosaurs and, much later, giant mammals such as woolly mammoths and saber-toothed cats. Some scientists believe we are living in a sixth mass extinction. Sudden and catastrophic changes to our planet (such as a massive asteroid crashing into Earth that rapidly altered global climate patterns) probably caused the previous extinctions. Other extinctions may have resulted from a changing climate over thousands of years. Species adapted to these new conditions, or they died out.

This new, sixth extinction is occurring at an alarming rate. And it is caused by human actions. Humans pollute the air and water. Humans hunt and poach animals such as rhinos and giraffes for body parts, pets, or trophies. Humans dam rivers, drain wetlands, and push farther into the wilderness to build roads, croplands, and cities.

Meanwhile, we rely on carbon-based fuels (petroleum, natural gas, and coal) to power our vehicles and our factories and to heat our homes and workplaces. These fuels release huge amounts of greenhouse gases, especially carbon dioxide (CO_2). These gases trap the sun's heat in Earth's atmosphere, creating a greenhouse effect. The result is a gradually warming atmosphere. Some predictions describe the average global temperature rising by 2.7°F (1.5°C) by the year 2100. Just a few degree's increase in atmospheric temperature can greatly alter worldwide weather patterns leading to megastorms, flooding, and rising sea levels in some areas, and drought, wildfire, and the expansion of inhospitable deserts in others.

With human misuse of Earth's resources paired with a rapidly changing climate, many species won't be able to adapt to these new environments. As a result, many species can no longer survive in their original habitats and are dying out. As we destroy more habitats, these species have fewer and fewer options. Extinction is closing in on many species.

The International Union for the Conservation of Nature (IUCN) is a worldwide group dedicated to conserving species under threat. Known as the Red List, the IUCN maintains a massive database that tracks the thousands of species around the world that are facing extinction. The IUCN says that the current rate of species loss might actually be worse than feared since only about 14 percent of species worldwide have been identified. Experts believe the current rate of extinction is one thousand to ten thousand times faster than a natural rate of extinction.

Extinction is forever, and this new rate of extinction threatens the very diversity of life on Earth. Around the world, scientists are working to understand the role of venomous animals in the natural world and how these mysteries can be used for good. If a snake, spider, or other venomous creature goes extinct, the cure for cancer or diabetes may vanish with it. Once we lose a species to extinction, it will never return.

In her office at the VIPER lab, Boyer still has boundless optimism. "There are lessons we can learn from venom that we cannot learn anywhere else," she says. "By just taking a molecule from a snake and studying it closely, we can invent things—drugs, tools, industrial chemicals . . . amazing science! And if we lose the biodiversity of venom we'll never even know what amazing things future inventors and scientists might have discovered."

SAVE A SNAKE

The IUCN Red List has classified many species of snakes as Near Threatened, Vulnerable, Endangered, or Critically Endangered. And many of these species' populations are declining as well. However, snakes are a critical part of the food chain. We need snakes, so how can we make sure they stick around?

- Educate yourself about the snake species found near your home. Find out whether they are venomous.
- Find out where snakes may live in your area. Avoid disturbing or destroying these habitats.
- Never kill a snake. If you encounter a snake, do not provoke it or move close to it. Wait quietly for the snake to recognize you are not a threat and move on. If you find a venomous snake near your home or yard, call a professional to remove the reptile.
- Spread the word about snakes. Help educate others about the snakes found in your area, how to avoid them, and what to do if you see a snake.
- Volunteer with a snake conservation organization. Many organizations work with citizen scientists to identify and record snakes found in an area. If you see a snake, take a picture and share your findings with the wildlife organization in your region.

VENOMOUS SNAKES OF THE UNITED STATES

This short guide includes a sampling of some of the more widespread venomous snakes that occur in the United States. For more details about these and other snakes, check out the Further Information section of this book.

EASTERN DIAMONDBACK RATTLESNAKE (*CROTALUS ADAMANTEUS*)

The largest of rattlers, the eastern diamondback rattlesnake can grow up to 8 feet (2.4 m). Like all rattlesnakes, this species is a carnivore, mostly consuming small mammals such as rodents. Adults have distinct dark diamond-shaped patterns along their backs. They are often found sharing burrows with the gopher tortoise (*Gopherus polyphemus*).

Range: southeastern states from North Carolina to Louisiana

Habitat: coastal lowlands, pine forests

Venom: high yield (amount of venom produced with one bite) with a mixture of toxins, deadly if not treated

WESTERN DIAMONDBACK RATTLESNAKE (*CROTALUS ATROX*)

The most common and widespread rattlesnake found in the southwestern states is also the largest rattler in the West. It is sometimes found in urban areas. Generally considered quick to strike, the species is credited with the most annual snakebite deaths in the United States.

Range: southern states from Arkansas to California

Habitat: varied; lowland desert to conifer forest

Venom: large yield of potent hemotoxins

MOJAVE RATTLESNAKE (*CROTALUS SCUTULATUS*)

This species has the most potent of all rattlesnake venoms. It is often confused with the western diamondback rattlesnake due to the two species' similar markings.

Range: Texas, New Mexico, Nevada, Arizona, and California

Habitat: mostly desert grasslands

Venom: high venom yield with a mixture of potent hemo- and neurotoxins

TIMBER RATTLESNAKE (*CROTALUS HORRIDUS*)

This is the most widespread venomous species in the eastern United States. Its appearance and venom composition may vary greatly depending on the geographic location. Also known as the canebrake or banded rattlesnake, this species is the third-largest rattlesnake species. Snake handlers in religious cult ceremonies often use this species, possibly because of its reluctance to strike.

Range: most of the eastern United States

Habitat: varied; upland deciduous forests to lowland swamps

Venom: high yield, highly toxic

YELLOW-BELLIED SEA SNAKE (*PELAMIS PLATURUS*)

The only sea snake found in American waters, this snake, also known as the pelagic sea snake, is often found in the open ocean. It has yellow coloring on its belly and, like other sea snakes, possesses an oar-shaped tail. It feeds almost exclusively on fish. This species is probably the most wide-ranging of all venomous snakes.

Range: Pacific and Indian Oceans

Habitat: open ocean, mostly tropical waters

Venom: small yield but highly toxic, mostly neuro- and myotoxins, which destroy muscle tissue

CORAL SNAKES

The United States is home to three species of coral snake: the Sonoran coral snake (*Micruroides euryxanthus*), the eastern coral snake (*Micrurus fulvius*), and the Texas coral snake (*Micrurus tener*). Coral snakes are the only elapid species native to the United States. All coral snakes are extremely colorful with varying bands of yellow, black, red, and white.

Range: three species ranging across much of the southern United States

Habitat: varied; higher elevation, rocky habitats in the Southwest to pine forest lowlands in the Southeast

Venom: small yield but possesses potent neurotoxins

COTTONMOUTH (*AGKISTRODON PISCIVORUS*)

Also called the water moccasin, the cottonmouth is mostly found near wetlands, especially in the southeastern United States. It gets its name from its defensive pose—a tight coil with its jaws flared open as if it has a mouth full of cotton.

Range: southeastern United States

Habitat: wetlands, rivers, and lakes

Venom: high yield and very toxic, capable of killing a human

COPPERHEAD (*AGKISTRODON CONTORTRIX*)

Along with the cottonmouth, the copperhead is part of a small group of common venomous snakes called moccasins. The copperhead gets its name from its striking copper-colored patterns, especially on its head.

Range: most of the eastern United States

Habitat: deciduous forests and other woodlands

Venom: low yield and low toxicity but can be highly destructive to the immediate area of the bite

SIDEWINDER (*CROTALUS CERASTES*)

Named for its unique form of locomotion, the sidewinder moves at an angle to reduce the surface area (parts of its belly) that touches the hot desert floor. The sidewinder often buries most of its body in loose sand to ambush prey. Distinct scales above the eyes are raised like horns.

Range: Arizona, Nevada, and California

Habitat: lowland dry desert, dunes, and creosote flats

Venom: low yield, low toxicity

MASSASSAUGA (*SISTRURUS CATENATUS*)

This species is timid and rarely strikes. It is one of only three rattlesnake species native to Canada. Due to habitat loss across its range, this species was listed as Threatened under the Endangered Species Act in 2016.

Range: Upper Midwest, Great Lakes region to Southwest

Habitat: varied; wetlands to arid grasslands

Venom: low yield but highly toxic

PYGMY RATTLESNAKE (*SISTRURUS MILIARIUS*)

As its name implies, this species is one of the smallest rattlesnake species, growing up to 24 inches (61 cm). It has a gray body with black-and-red markings along its back.

Range: much of the southeastern United States

Habitat: pine woodlands and grassy wetlands

Venom: low yield but possesses strong hemotoxins

SOURCE NOTES

6 Leslie Boyer, MD, VIPER Institute, personal interviews with the author, February–June 2017.

7 Boyer.

12 Boyer.

15 Boyer.

25 Stephane Poulin, Arizona-Sonora Desert Museum, personal interview with the author, June 2017.

28 Poulin.

46 Dr. Alejandro Alagón, Universidad Nacional Autónoma de México, personal interview with the author, April 2017.

49–50 Alagón.

54 Christopher Ingraham, "This $153,000 Rattlesnake Bite is Everything Wrong with American Health Care," *The Washington Post*, July 20, 2015, https://www.washingtonpost.com/news/wonk/wp/2015/07/20/this-153000-rattlesnake-bite-is-everything-wrong-with-american-health-care/?utm_term=.6108b02e8bc2.

72 Boyer.

75 Boyer.

79 Boyer.

79 Boyer.

79 Boyer.

87 Boyer.

GLOSSARY

angiotensin-converting enzyme (ACE) inhibitor: pharmaceutical drugs that help relax blood vessels and treat hypertension (high blood pressure)

antibodies: large proteins found in plasma that neutralize bacteria, viruses, and toxins

antigen: a toxin or other foreign substance that creates an immune response

antivenom: also known as antivenin, medication used to treat venomous bites and stings

binomial nomenclature: a naming system in which two Latin words identify an individual species

biome: a large community of plants and animals that occupy a region, such as a desert, tundra, or deciduous forest

capitalist: practicing the economic system based on private ownership and pursuit of profits

climate change: change in global climate patterns, mostly attributed to an increase in fossil fuel use, which emits greenhouse gases

coevolution: two or more species living in the same ecosystem that adapt alongside one another and whose actions affect one another

crypsis: the ability of an animal to avoid detection, such as by using camouflage

deciduous: referring to a tree that sheds its leaves annually

deoxyribonucleic acid (DNA): a molecule that carries genetic information of cells that define growth, development, and function

ectothermic: an animal that relies on external sources such as the sun to regulate body temperature

energetics: the study of energy and how it is redistributed in physical, chemical, and biological processes

envenomate: to poison by venom

epidemic: an outbreak of disease that spreads quickly and affects many people

Fab fragments: a part of an antibody that binds to an antigen such as a toxin molecule

genetics: the study of heredity or the variation of inherited characteristics

hemotoxin: toxins found in venom that destroy red blood cells, disrupt blood clotting, or destroy other tissue

immunity: the ability of an organism to resist infection

metabolism: the chemical processes that occur within an organism to maintain bodily functions

natural selection: a theory first described by Charles Darwin, in which organisms better adapted to their environment tend to survive and have offspring

nematocyst: specialized cells in jellyfish tentacles that contain a venomous barb

neuron: a specialized cell that transmits nerve impulses

neurotoxin: a toxic chemical found in venom that attacks nerve tissue and disrupts nervous system function

neurotransmitter: a chemical signal used by neurons to transmit impulses across a synapse, or the junction between two neurons

organism: an individual living thing

outbreak: a sudden rise in cases of a disease

paralysis: complete or partial loss of muscle function

pepsin: an enzyme in the stomach that digests proteins

peptide: a chain of amino acids (organic groups of carbon, hydrogen, and other elements) linked by bonds. Many amino acids together create a protein.

pharmaceutical: relating to the production and sale of drugs or medicine

phylum: a taxonomic classification that is the primary division of kingdoms. For example, snakes belong to the phylum Chordata, along with other animals possessing spinal columns.

plasma: the watery portion of blood in which blood cells and platelets are suspended

poisonous: capable of causing illness or death to a living organism when absorbed or introduced

predation: an ecological interaction where a predator feeds on prey for food

primate: an order of mammals, characterized by binocular vision, use of hands, complex social behaviors, and intelligence, including great apes, gibbons, monkeys, and humans

prosthetic: an artificial body part

protein: a large molecule containing carbon, hydrogen, oxygen, nitrogen, and sulfur linked together. Protein is essential for diet, metabolism, and other basic functions to maintain life.

serum: the liquid portion of blood plasma that contains proteins

shock: a critical medical condition, usually following a serious injury, where not enough blood reaches vital organs. It can result in serious damage and even death.

subsidize: to support financially

taxonomy: the system of classifying living things based on natural relationships

toxicology: the study of toxic chemicals such as poison and venom and their effects on other living organisms

toxin: a substance, usually protein, that can cause illness, injury, and even death when introduced to another living organism. Toxins often are found in poisons and venoms from plants and animals.

vaccine: a commercially produced weakened antigen introduced to the body to stimulate an immune response

venom: a toxic substance that can cause injury or even death when introduced to another organism through a bite or sting

venomics: the study of venom, especially understanding the venom molecule's profile and characteristics

viable: able to develop and survive

SELECTED BIBLIOGRAPHY

Alirol, Emilie, Pauline Lechevalier, Federica Zamatto, François Chappuis, Gabriel Alcoba, and Julien Potet. "Antivenoms for Snakebite Envenoming: What Is in the Research Pipeline?" *PLOS Neglected Tropical Diseases* 9, no. 9 (September 2015): e0003896. https://doi10.1371/journal.pntd.0003896.

Arnold, Carrie. "The Snakebite Fight." *Nature* 537 (September 2016): 26–28.

Beck, Daniel. "Ecology and Energetics of Three Sympatric Rattlesnake Species in the Sonoran Desert." *Journal of Herpetology* 29, no. 2 (June 1995): 211–223.

Bénard-Valle, M, E. E. Neri-Castro, B. G. Fry, L. Boyer, C. Cochran, M. Alam, T. N. W. Jackson, D. Paniagua, F. Olvera-Rodriguez, I. Koludarov, K. Sunagar, and A. Alagón. "Antivenom Research and Development." In *Venomous Reptiles and Their Toxins: Evolution, Pathophysiology, and Biodiscovery*, edited by Bryan G. Fry. Oxford: Oxford University Press, 2015, 61–72.

Berkrot, Bill. "Success Rate for Experimental Drugs Falls: Study." Reuters. Accessed June 30, 2017. http://www.reuters.com/article/us-pharmaceuticals-success -idUSTRE71D2U920110214.

Boyer, L. "On 1000-Fold Pharmaceutical Price Markups and Why Drugs Cost More in the United States Than in Mexico." *American Journal of Medicine* 128, no. 12 (December 2015): 1265–1267.

Boyer, L., A. Alagón, B. G. Fry, T. N.W. Jackson, K. Sunagar, and J.-P. Chippaux. "Signs, Symptoms, and Treatment of Envenomation." In *Venomous Reptiles and Their Toxins: Evolution, Pathophysiology, and Biodiscovery*, edited by Bryan G. Fry. Oxford: Oxford University Press, 2015, 32–60.

Brown, Nicholas I. "Consequences of Neglect: Analysis of the Sub-Saharan African Snake Antivenom Market and the Global Context." *PLOS Neglected Tropical Diseases* 6, no. 6 (June 5, 2012): e1670. https://doi.org/10.1371/journal.pntd.0001670.

Chippaux, Jean-Philippe. "Estimating the Global Burden of Snakebite Can Help to Improve Management." *PLOS Medicine* 5, no. 11 (November 4, 2008): e 221. https://doi.org/10.1371/journal.pmed.0050221.

———. "Snakebite in Africa: Current Situation and Urgent Needs." In *Handbook of Venoms and Toxins of Reptiles*, edited by Stephen P. Mackessy. Boca Raton, FL: CRC, 2009, 445–465.

———. "Snake-Bites: Appraisal of the Global Situation." *Bulletin of the World Health Organization* 76, no. 5 (1998): 515–524.

Chowell, G., J. M. Hyman, P. Díaz-Dueñas, and N. W. Hengartner. "Predicting Scorpion Sting Incidence in an Endemic Region Using Climatological Variables." *International Journal of Environmental Health Research* 15, no. 6 (December 2005): 425–435.

Columbus, Courtney. "Snakebites Make the List of 'Neglected Tropical Diseases.' " *NPR*, June 24, 2017. http://www.npr.org/sections/goastandsoda/2017/06/24/534134069 /snakebites-make-the-list-of-neglected-tropical-diseases.

Fry, Bryan G., ed. *Venomous Reptiles and Their Toxins: Evolution, Pathophysiology, and Biodiscovery*. Oxford: Oxford University Press, 2015.

Gandhi, Lakshmi. "A History of 'Snake Oil Salesmen.' " *NPR*, August 26, 2013. http://www.npr.org/sections/codeswitch/2013/08/26/215761377/a-history-of-snake -oil-salesmen.

Gutiĕrrrez, J. M., D. A. Warrell, D. J. Williams, S. Jensen, N. Brown, J. J. Calvete, and R. A. Harrison. "The Need for Full Integration of Snakebite Envenoming within a Global Strategy to Combat the Neglected Tropical Diseases: The Way Forward." *PLOS Neglected Tropical Diseases* 7, no. 6 (2013): e2162.

Ingraham, Christopher. "This $153,000 Rattlesnake Bite Is Everything Wrong with American Health Care." *Washington Post, Wonkblog*, July 20, 2015. https://www .washingtonpost.com/news/wonk/wp/2015/07/20/this-153000-rattlesnake-bite-is -everything-wrong-with-american-health-care/?utm_term=.b3c9e7d5dfce.

Isbell, Lynne A. "Snakes as Agents of Evolutionary Change in Primate Brain." *Journal of Human Evolution* 51 (July 2006): 1–35.

Ivanyi, Craig. *A Natural History of the Sonoran Desert*. Edited by Steven J. Phillips and Patricia Wentworth Comus. Tucson: Arizona-Sonora Desert Museum Press; Berkeley: University of California Press, 2000.

Kasturiratne, Anuradhani, A. Rajitha Wickremasinghe, Nilanthi de Silva, N. Kithsiri Gunawardena, Arunasalam Pathmeswaran, Ranjan Premaratna, Lorenzo Savioli, David G. Lalloo, and H. Janaka de Silva. "The Global Burden of Snakebite: A Literature Analysis and Modelling Based on Regional Estimates of Envenoming and Deaths." *PLOS Medicine* 5, no. 11 (November 4, 2008): e 218. https://doi .org/10.1371/journal.pmed.0050218.

Kipanyula, M. J., and W. H. Kimaro. "Snakes and Snakebite Envenoming in Northern Tanzania: A Neglected Tropical Health Problem." *Journal of Venomous Animals and Toxins Including Tropical Diseases* 21 (2015): 32.

Kliff, Sarah. "8 Facts That Explain What's Wrong with American Health Care." *Vox*, September 2, 2014. Available online at Physicians for a National Health Program. http://www.pnhp.org/news/2014/september/8-facts-that-explain-what%E2%80%99s -wrong-with-american-health-care.

Kumar, Sheila V. "Snakes' Expanding Habitat Could Bring Their Venom to Surprising Places." *Inside Climate News,* March 2, 2016. https://insideclimatenews .org/print/42466.

Lewis, Danny. "Why a Single Vial of Antivenom Can Cost $14,000." *Smithsonian. com*, September 11, 2015. https://www.smithsonianmag.com/smart-news/why-single -vial-antivenom-can-cost-14000-180956564/.

Murphy, John C. *Secrets of the Snake Charmer: Snakes in the 21st Century.* Bloomington, IN: iUniverse, 2010.

Nori, Javier, Paola A. Carrasco, and Gerardo C. Leynaud. "Venomous Snakes and Climate Change: Ophidism as a Dynamic Problem." *Climate Change* 122 (December 2013). https://doi.org/10.1007/s10584-013-1019-6.

Ossola, Alexandra. "10 Crazy Uses for Animal Venom." *Popular Science*, March 17, 2015. http://www.popsci.com/10-crazy-uses-animal-venom.

Rakison, D. H., and J. Derringer. "Do Infants Possess an Evolved Spider-Detection Mechanism?" *Cognition* 107, no. 1 (April 2008): 381–393.

Sanders, Laura. "Venom Hunters." *Science News*, August 15, 2009. https://www.sciencenews.org/article/venom-hunters?mode=magazine&context=688.

Santibáñez-López, C. E., O. F. Francke, C. Ureta, and L. D. Possani. "Scorpions from Mexico: From Species Diversity to Venom Complexity." *Toxins* 8, no. 1 (December 2015): 2.

Simpson, I. D. "Time for an Alternative Perspective: The Eternal Problem of Supply and Quality of Anti Snake Venom in the Developing World—'It's the Economy, Stupid.'" *Wilderness and Environmental Medicine* 19, no. 3 (Fall 2008): 186–194.

Simpson, I. D., and R. S. Blaylock. "The Anti Snake Venom Crisis in Africa: A Suggested Manufacturers Product Guide." *Wilderness and Environmental Medicine* 20, no. 3 (Fall 2009): 275–282.

Simpson, I. D., and R. L. Norris. "The Global Snakebite Crisis—a Public Health Issue Misunderstood, Not Neglected." *Wilderness and Environmental Medicine* 20, no. 1 (Spring 2009): 43–56.

———. "Snake Antivenom Product Guidelines in India: 'The Devil Is in the Details.'" *Wilderness and Environmental Medicine* 18, no. 3 (Fall 2007): 163–168.

———. "Snakes of Medical Importance in India: Is the Concept of the 'Big 4' Still Relevant and Useful?" *Wilderness Environmental Medicine* 18, no. 1 (Spring 2008): 2–9.

"Snakebites in Africa: Challenges and Solution." Kofi Annan Foundation meeting, Geneva, December 13, 2016. http://www.kofiannanfoundation.org/app/uploads/2016/12/Snakebites-in-Africa-Meeting-Final-Report.pdf.

Solomon, E .P., L. R. Berg, and D. W. Martin. *Biology*, 8th ed. Belmont, CA: Thomson Brooks/Cole, 2008.

Theakston, R. D. G., and D. A. Warrell. "Crisis in Snake Antivenom Supply for Africa." *Lancet* 356, no. 9247 (December 16, 2000). https://doi.org/10.1016/S0140-6736(05)74319-1.

Thomas, David W., Justin Burns, John Audette, Adam Carroll, Corey Dow-Hygelund, and Michael Hay. "Clinical Development Success Rates, 2006–2015." Biotechnology Innovation Organization. Accessed July 4, 2017. https://www.bio.org/sites/default

/files/Clinical%20Development%20Success%20Rates%202006-2015%20-%20
BIO,%20Biomedtracker,%20Amplion%202016.pdf.

Ungar, Rick. "The Great American Hospital Pricing Scam Exposed—We Now Know
Why Healthcare Costs Are So Artificially High." *Forbes*, May 8, 2013. https://www
.forbes.com/sites/rickungar/2013/05/08/the-great-american-hospital-pricing-scam
-exposed-we-now-know-why-healthcare-costs-are-so-artificially-high/#21912b273bff.

Utkin, Yuri N. "Animal Venom Studies: Current Benefits and Future Developments."
World Journal of Biological Chemistry 6, no. 2 (May 26, 2016): 28–33.

"Venomous Snakes Distribution and Species Risk Categories." World Health
Organization. Accessed May 5, 2017. http://apps.who.int/bloodproducts
/snakeantivenoms/database.

Visser, L. E., S. Kyei-Faried, and D. W. Belcher. "Protocol and Monitoring to Improve
Snake Bite Outcomes in Rural Ghana." *Transactions of the Royal Society of Tropical
Medicine and Hygiene* 98, no. 5 (May 2004): 278–283.

Visser, L. E., S. Kyei-Faried, D. W. Belcher, D. W. Geelhoed, J. Schagen van
Leeuwen, and J. van Roosmalen. "Failure of a New Antivenom to Treat *Echis ocellatus*
Snake Bite in Rural Ghana: The Importance of Quality Surveillance." *Transactions of
the Royal Society of Tropical Medicine and Hygiene* 102, no. 5 (May 2008): 445–450.
https://www. doi.org/ 10.1016/j.trstmh.2007.11.006.

Wade, Lizzie. "For Mexican Antivenom Maker, U.S. Market Is a Snake Pit." *Science
Magazine* 343, no. 3 (January 2014): 16–17.

*WHO Guidelines for the Production, Control, and Regulation of Snake Antivenom
Immunoglobulins*. World Health Organization, May 2010. https://www.who.int
/bloodproduct/snake_antivenoms/snakeantivenomguide/en/.

Wilcox, Christie. "Another Reason to Act Now on Climate Change: Snakes." *Science
Sushi, Discover*, March 31, 2016. http://blogs.discovermagazine.com/science
-sushi/2016/03/31/climate-change-may-worsen-snakebite/#.WYiWMq2ZPp4.

———. "Poison as Medicine." *Discover*, March 24, 2015. http://discovermagazine
.com/2015/april/00-poison-medicine.

Williams, D. J., José-Maria Gutiérrez, J. J. Calvete, W. Wüster, K. Ratanabanangkoon,
O. Paiva, N. I. Brown, N. R. Casewell, R. A. Harrison, P. D. Rowley, M. O'Shea,
S. D. Jensen, K. D. Winkel, and D. A. Warrell. "Ending the Drought: New Strategies
for Improving the Flow of Affordable, Effective Antivenoms in Asia and Africa."
Journal of Protemic 74, no. 9 (August 24, 2011): 1735–1767.

World Health Organization. *Guidelines for the Prevention and Clinical Management of
Snakebite in Africa*. Brazzaville, Republic of the Congo: WHO, 2010.

FURTHER INFORMATION

Books

Collins, Joseph T. *A Field Guide to Reptiles and Amphibians: Eastern and Central North America*, 4th ed. New York: Houghton Mifflin Harcourt, 2016.
This book, available for eastern and western states, is the definitive guide for identifying reptiles and amphibians in the field.

Downer, Ann. *The Animal Mating Game: The Wacky, Weird World of Sex in the Animal Kingdom*. Minneapolis: Twenty-First Century Books, 2017.
This fun, informative, and visually engaging book explores the wide world of animal reproduction. Learn about the life cycles, courting, and mating habits of a range of animals, from hyenas, bats, and penguins to spiders, frogs, and snakes.

————. *Wild Animal Neighbors: Sharing Our Urban World*. Minneapolis: Twenty-First Century Books, 2016.
This colorful and engaging book explores some of the conflicts and solutions for living in harmony with our wild neighbors as humans expand into their habitats.

Fry, Bryan Grieg. *Venom Doc: The Edgiest, Darkest, Strangest Natural History Memoir Ever*. New York: Arcade, 2016.
Read the personal story of Bryan Grieg Fry, one of the world's authorities on all things venomous. This book introduces his fascinating work with dangerous species around the world.

Hirsch, Rebecca E. *De-Extinction: The Science of Bringing Lost Species Back to Life*. Minneapolis: Twenty-First Century Books, 2017.
Learn about scientific efforts to reintroduce extinct animals, including woolly mammoths, passenger pigeons, bucardos, and dodo birds.

Lillywhite, Harvey B. *How Snakes Work: Structure, Function, and Behavior of the World's Snakes*. New York: Oxford University Press, 2014.
Through an accessible combination of academic research and popular science writing, this book covers everything about snakes, from their evolutionary history to their anatomy and ecology.

Rosen, Michael J. *Outrageous Animal Adaptations: From Big-Eared Bats to Frill-Necked Lizards*. Minneapolis: Twenty-First Century Books, 2018.
This engaging book offers intriguing information about animal adaptations and evolution across the natural world. Readers will learn about land and aquatic animals, including mudskippers, vampire squids, naked mole rats, and frill-necked lizards.

Rubio, Manny. *Guide to the Rattlesnakes of the United States and Canada*. Rodeo, NM: ECO Books, 2010.
Filled with beautiful photographs, this book covers identification of rattlers, their natural history, and much more.

Shupe, Scott. *Venomous Snakes and Their Mimics*. New York: Skyhorse, 2011.
This authoritative author provides an excellent guide to the venomous snakes of North America, complete with full-color maps and photographs.

Shupe, Scott, and the Department of the Navy Bureau of Medicine and Surgery. *Venomous Snakes of the World: A Manual for Use by U.S. Amphibious Forces*. New York: Skyhorse, 2013.
Used by U.S. military forces around the world, this is the definitive guide to nearly three hundred species of venomous snakes.

Wilcox, Christie. *Venomous: How Earth's Deadliest Creatures Mastered Biochemistry*. New York; Scientific America/Farrar, Straus and Giroux, 2016.
Written by a biochemist, this book is a fun and accessible journey through the world of venomous creatures.

Films and Videos

African Society of Venimology: Snakebite and Treatment in Sub-Saharan Africa
https://vimeo.com/channels/venimology
Watch these videos produced by the African Society of Venimology to learn more about snakebite and the vicious circle in sub-Saharan Africa.

Cohen, Chad. "Venom: Nature's Killer," *NOVA*. PBS, February 23, 2011.
This 2011 PBS documentary explores the world of venomous snakes and how their deadly potion is used in the medical industry.

Deadliest Snakes Living in Africa. National Geographic BBC Wild Documentary, 2016. https://youtu.be/2ck0m3J6ts4.
Produced by *National Geographic*, this documentary uses spellbinding footage to investigate the Elapidae family of venomous snakes.

Morgan, Ray. *The Venom Interviews: The Work and Science of Venomous Herpetology*. Code Rica Media, Inc., 2017. http://thevenominterviews.com.
This documentary series about venomous snakes features many interviews with the world's leading snake researchers, including Leslie Boyer and Bryan Fry, among others.

PBS Nature: Snakes
http://www.pbs.org/wnet/nature/group/amphibians-reptiles/snake/
This page offers short clips and full episodes of PBS's acclaimed *Nature* series that specifically focus on snakes.

Reid, James, and Philip Gilmour. *Minutes to Die: The World's Ignored Health Crisis*. Directed by James Reid and Philip Gilmour, 2017. http://minutestodie.com/the-snakebite-crisis/.
This 2017 feature film is a moving documentary that takes viewers to five continents to meet the people and communities affected by the snakebite crisis.

Websites

Discover Life
http://www.discoverlife.org/mp/20q?guide=Snakes
Use this resource to learn how to identify snakes and many other types of animals.

Global Snakebite Initiative
http://www.snakebiteinitiative.org/
Learn more about the snakebite crisis. The site includes information about the prevalence of snakebites around the world as well as resources about venomous snakes and the people fighting the snakebite crisis.

International Union for the Conservation of Nature (IUCN) Red List
http://www.iucnredlist.org
This authoritative database gives information including endangerment status about many of the world's species.

Leslie Boyer MD (Blog)
https://scorpiondoc.silvrback.com
In Leslie Boyer's personal blog, she uses her personal experiences to give insights into the world of venomous creatures and development of antivenoms.

National Institutes for Occupational Safety and Health: Venomous Snakes
https://www.cdc.gov/niosh/topics/snakes/default.html
Learn about venomous snakes, symptoms of snakebites, and first aid techniques.

Texas Parks & Wildlife: Venomous Snake Safety
https://tpwd.texas.gov/education/resources/texas-junior-naturalists/be-nature-safe/venomous-snake-safety
Find out about North America's most common venomous snakes, and learn about snake safety.

VIPER Institute
http://viper.arizona.edu/
Learn the latest news about antivenoms and venomous organisms from publications, videos, and more.

World Health Organization: Snakebite Envenoming
http://www.who.int/mediacentre/factsheets/fs337/en
Read more about the snakebite crisis from the World Health Organization with the latest data, published reports, and links to many other resources.

INDEX

ABOUT THE AUTHOR

Charles C. Hofer is a wildlife biologist, photographer, and writer living in Tucson, Arizona, home to many, many venomous snakes. He has been a regular contributor to several award-winning magazines, where he often writes about science and nature for young minds. This is his first book for young adults.

PHOTO ACKNOWLEDGMENTS

Image credits: EkaterinaP/Shutterstock.com (background). Tim Flach/Stone/ Getty Images, p. 1; Anthony Pappone/Moment/Getty Images, p. 5; Courtesy of the Author, pp. 6, 11, 25, 44, 45, 46, 49, 50, 51, 77Irfan Khan/Los Angeles Times/ Getty Images, p. 9; ISAAC KASAMANI/AFP/Getty Images, p. 10; Laura Westlund/ Independent Picture Service, pp. 13, 21, 37, 76; Ferdy Timmerman/Shutterstock. com, p. 17; Richard Ellis/Alamy Stock Photo, p. 18; Rex Lisman/Moment/Getty Images, pp. 21 (left), 90 (top); Kristian Bell/Shutterstock.com, p. 21 (right); Tom Uhlman/Alamy Stock Photo, p. 22; tunart/iStock/Getty Images Plus/Getty Images, p. 24; PATTARAWIT CHOMPIPAT/Alamy Stock Photo, p. 26; Shoemcfly/iStock/ Getty Images Plus/Getty Images, p. 28; Merlot Levert/Shutterstock.com, p. 31; corlaffra/Shutterstock.com, p. 32; Byronsdad/E+/Getty Images, p. 33; Dirk Ercken/ Shutterstock.com, p. 34; Xinhua/Alamy Stock Photo, p. 39; Rex Lisman/Royalty- free/Getty Images, p. 40; Utopia_88/Shutterstock.com, p. 42; Hulton Archive/Getty Images, p. 48; Gamma-Keystone/Getty Images, p. 52; Courtesy of the Author, p. 53; Ryan M. Bolton/Shutterstock.com, p. 55; Wikimedia Commons (pubiic domain), p. 63; imageBROKER/Alamy Stock Photo, p. 67; age fotostock/Alamy Stock Photo, p. 69; Archivo Agencia EL UNIVERSAL/RML/Newscom, p. 70; Allison Joyce/Getty Images, p. 73; Andrea Sicuri/EyeEm/Getty Images, p. 78; JohnPitche/iStock/Getty Images, p. 81; AFP PHOTO/Mauricio LIMA/Getty Images, p. 83; jokerbethyname/ Shutterstock.com, p. 88 (top); Matt Jeppson/Shutterstock.com, p. 88 (middle); SteveByland/iStock/Getty Images, p. 88 (bottom); Danita Delimont/Alamy Stock Photo, p. 89; Maciej Bogusz/Shutterstock.com, p. 89 (middle); John Cancalos/age fotostock/Getty Images, p. 89 (bottom); © Rich Reid/National Geographic Stock, p. 90 (bottom); © George Grall/National Geographic Stock, p. 91 (middle); Matt Jeppson/Shutterstock.com, p. 91 (top); Nature's Images/Science Source/Getty Images, p. 91 (bottom).

Cover: DedeDian/Shutterstock.com (blue snake); Byronsdad/E+/Getty Images (tan snake); EkaterinaP/Shutterstock.com (background).